CARMELITE STUDIES

IX

CARMELITE STUDIES

THE HEIRS OF
ST. TERESA OF ÁVILA:
DEFENDERS AND DISSEMINATORS
OF THE FOUNDING
MOTHER'S LEGACY

Edited by Christopher C. Wilson

ICS Publications
Institute of Carmelite Studies
Washington, DC

Edizioni Carmelitane
Institutum Carmelitanum
Rome, Italy

2006

ICS Publications
2131 Lincoln Road, NE
Washington, DC 20002-1199
www.icspublications.org

Typeset and produced in the United States of America

Library of Congress Cataloging-in-Publication Data

The heirs of St. Teresa of Ávila : defenders and disseminators of the founding
Mother's legacy / edited by Christopher C. Wilson.
  p. cm. -- (Carmelite studies),
  Includes bibliographical references.
  ISBN 0-935216-40-5 (alk. paper)
  1. Discalced Carmelite nuns--Spain--Biography. 2. Discalced Carmelite nuns--
Spain--History. 3. Teresa, of Ávila, Saint, 1515-1582. I. Wilson, Christopher
Chadwick. II. Series.
  BX4308.Z7H45 2006
  271 .971046--dc22
               2006003576

Contents

Introduction

Writing nearly half a century ago, Winifred Nevin began her 1959 book *Heirs of St. Teresa of Ávila* with an explanation of its title: "Heirs of Teresa of Ávila are all members of the Discalced Carmelite Order, but in this case the designation refers to those who were St. Teresa's own particular choice: those whom she singled out for special instruction; on whose talents, virtues, and fidelity to the spirit that quickened the Reform she based her hope for its continuance and increase." This issue of *Carmelite Studies* echoes Nevin's title and theme. The essays collected here present new insights into the lives and writings of those individuals who knew Teresa in life and who, after her death in 1582, worked to propagate and defend her legacy, including four of her most illustrious nuns, Ana de San Bartolomé, Ana de Jesús, María de San José, and Ana de San Agustín, and her close male confidante and collaborator, Jerónimo Gracián de la Madre de Dios. Each deserving of greater scholarly attention, these figures are here given precedence over St. John of the Cross, another unique and prolific "heir," since he has already been the subject of an extensive bibliography. A further focus of the essays is the reception of the Teresian heritage by individuals outside the order, as mediated by these early Discalced Carmelites and by Teresa's published writings.

The essays were originally presented at the 2004 symposium "The Heirs of St. Teresa" at Georgetown University. That year marked the 400th anniversary of a pivotal moment in Discalced Carmelite history: the arrival in France of a group of six nuns, some of Teresa's most favored protégées, including Ana de Jesús and Ana de San Bartolomé, who had traveled from Spain to inaugurate the order's first French convent. For readers today, far removed from the religious wars that pitted Catholic against Huguenot in sixteenth-century France and the subsequent Catholic renewal born from these eruptions, it may be difficult to recover the gravity of the occasion. The nuns perceived the venture as no less than a culmination of Teresa's project of religious reform since, during her life, France was very much on her mind. In the prologue to *The Way of Perfection* Teresa explains that she founded her first convent, St. Joseph's in Ávila, with "so much external austerity" because "news reached me of the harm being done in France and of the havoc those Lutherans [the term by which Teresa refers to Huguenots] had caused and how much this miserable sect was growing."[1] Through unceasing prayer and rigorous observance of what she understood as the primitive Carmelite rule, Teresa insisted, her nuns could assist the Church's efforts and counteract further loss of souls. Ana de San Bartolomé wrote that Teresa's intention was that "all those who would join her monasteries should be always engaged in prayer and holy exercises of mortification and penance, in order to aid Jesus Christ and His Catholics in the conversion of the kingdom of France. This country was so continually present to her thoughts, and she wished earnestly for its salvation, that she did not cease to cry to God in order to obtain it."[2] By founding convents in France and later in the Spanish Netherlands, Teresa's nuns believed that they were taking the next necessary step in supporting a Church in crisis. Due in large part to the determined (and sometimes contested) leadership of the Spanish *Madres*, the order took hold there and spread rapidly: by 1615 ten convents had been founded in France; by 1620, twenty-seven; and by 1625, thirty-seven.[3]

Also in 1604, the same year that the Spanish nuns arrived in Paris, another significant expansion occurred across the Atlantic when the first Discalced Carmelite convent in the Americas was founded in the Mexican city of Puebla. Since Teresa intended for her nuns' prayers and mortifications to be directed toward the work of conversion of Native Americans as well as Protestants, the growth of her order within the New Word had special resonance.[4] Through prayer, dispensation of spiritual advice, acceptance of novices, and the placement of churches beside their convents, female monastic communities played a key role in cultivating a relatively young American Church. The propagation of Teresa's legacy, therefore, was a global enterprise.

In the past half-century several important publications, some authored by contributors to this volume, have encouraged new interest in Teresa's heirs. These include Julián Urkiza's magisterial critical edition of the works of Ana de San Bartolomé; Ildefonso Moriones' study of Ana de Jesús; Joseph Chorpenning's anthology of readings from Jerónimo Gracián's *Summary of the Excellencies of St. Joseph,* with its introductory analysis of Gracián's life and work; and Elizabeth Teresa Howe's edition of two autobiographical *relaciones* by Ana de San Agustín (*The Visionary Life of Madre Ana de San Agustín*). Of particular significance is the pioneering1989 anthology by Electa Arenal and Stacey Schlau, *Untold Sisters: Hispanic Nuns in Their Own Works,* which contains selections by Ana de San Bartolomé and María de San José. For many readers in the United States (including myself), this volume provided an initial acquaintance with the writings of Teresa's daughters. A more recent anthology by Barbara Mujica, *Women Writers of Early Modern Spain: Sofia's Daughters,* attests to continued enthusiasm for these two nuns through its inclusion of some of their written works. Alison Weber has greatly expanded our knowledge of and appreciation for María de San José with her edition of *Book for the Hour of Recreation,* with translations by Amanda Powell and an introductory essay investigating María's role in the Carmelite reform and her literary contributions.[5]

The present volume begins with Weber concentrating further on

María de San José, here chronicling the steps by which she learned a lesson in discipleship. Soon after Teresa appointed her as prioress of the new Seville convent, María had to manage disruption within the community when two nuns began to report mystical experiences of dubious authenticity. She complained that the convent's confessor and chaplain fueled the unhealthy situation. Through letters Teresa counseled María to handle the affair with patience, courtesy, and tolerance for the weakness of others but was often frustrated by her young protégée's headstrong attitude. María's subsequent writings reveal that she eventually absorbed Teresa's example of gentleness in negotiations with others.

Barbara Mujica explores Teresa's complex relationship with another strong-willed personality within the reform, Jerónimo Gracián de la Madre de Dios. Scholars have long been puzzled by the saint's deep friendship—some would even say infatuation—with the young, impetuous friar whom she met in 1575 and to whom she almost immediately made a spontaneous vow of obedience. Mujica analyzes Teresa's correspondence with Gracián and suggests that, though she professed obedience to him, she took on the role of fond mother who sometimes treated her spiritual son with indulgence, and at other times tried to supervise him with directives and reprimands.

In order to show how Teresa's nuns often invoked the foundress in order to shore up their own claims to authority, Elizabeth Teresa Howe examines the autobiographical writings (*relaciones*) of Ana de San Agustín, a nun whom Teresa recruited to accompany her to the new foundation at Villanueva de la Jara and who later was elected prioress of that community. Her writings are replete with accounts of mystical experiences, including her visions of heaven and hell. She also claimed to receive posthumous visits and instructions from Teresa that authorized her own role as mediator between the deceased foundress and those on earth who had not personally known her.

Kieran Kavanaugh concentrates on Ana de San Bartolomé (Anne of St. Bartholomew), the constant companion of Teresa's final years, who spent the last decades of her life spreading the Carmelite reform in France and the Spanish Netherlands. Kavanaugh explores the founding of the first French Discalced Carmelite convents and considers conflicts that arose over the thorny issue of jurisdiction. Three secular clerics—Messieurs Duval, Gallement, and Bérulle—had been appointed as the nuns' superiors. The Spanish nuns believed that these men would govern the order only until Discalced Carmelite friars were established in France. The three French clerics, though, had obtained a papal bull perpetuating their own rule over the order's spiritual affairs. A resulting crisis of authority ensued, during which Ana de San Bartolomé struggled with her French superiors (especially Pierre de Bérulle) in order to defend her vision of the Teresian ideal.

My own essay investigates how visual representations of Ana de San Bartolomé and Ana de Jesús were used to champion the posthumous cults—or, as I argue, the rival cults —of each nun in the Spanish Netherlands, where they both died. Engravings and paintings promoted public devotion to the two Anas and encouraged momentum toward what was hoped would be their eventual beatification and canonization. Though images emphasize the exceptionality of each Ana, casting her as the privileged successor to the Founding Mother's authority, they share the common purpose of identifying both as potent defenders of the Counter-Reformation Church.

The final two essays expand the volume's scope through investigation of Teresa's legacy outside the Discalced Carmelite Order. Jodi Bilinkoff considers the many ways that readers across Catholic Europe and the New World responded to and utilized Teresa's written works. She provides widely varied examples of women and men, lay and religious, Carmelites and members of other orders, who found in Teresa's writings "guidance, consolation, and strategies for coping with personal problems." Her study reveals that, for many early modern readers, Teresa was a gauge by which to measure their own spiritual progress.

One enthusiastic reader of Teresa's best-selling books was St. Francis de Sales, the subject of Joseph Chorpenning's essay. Francis referred to the saint as "Notre chère Mère Thérèse," and, in his *Treatise on the Love of God,* declares that "in all those books of hers we are filled with admiration at her eloquent humility, her intelligence and simplicity."[6] Motivated by his empathy for Teresian spirituality, Francis assisted with the introduction of the Discalced Carmelite Order into France. Like Teresa, he assigned a privileged position to St. Joseph in his spirituality. Chorpenning investigates parallels and differences in the two saints' experiences of and writings about Joseph, considering ways that both helped shape early modern perceptions of the earthly father of Christ. The essays by Bilinkoff and Chorpenning demonstrate that Teresa had countless heirs who, though they did not know her in life, nevertheless felt a strong kinship with her through reading her books.

An overarching theme that emerges in the essays is the problem of competing claims to authority. Nuns who had worked with Teresa understandably felt that their discipleship gave them a natural leadership status within the order and a responsibility to carry out what they interpreted as Teresa's wishes. Their own self-perception as defenders of the Teresian legacy, reaffirmed by mystical experiences (such as the reception of posthumous visits from the saint), sometimes put them at odds with male prelates. Such tensions arose even before Teresa's death, as Weber demonstrates in her discussion of the standoff between María de San José and Garciálvarez, the chaplain and principal confessor of the Seville Carmel, over the prioress' role in spiritual direction. But the inherent conflict between nuns' inherited authority and patriarchal institutional authority is best (or perhaps most sadly) illustrated by the 1590 episode known as "the nuns' revolt" which is referenced throughout the essays. Nicolás Doria, elected provincial of the order in 1585, proposed changes in monastic governance and sought to alter the original Teresian constitutions, including downsizing the office of prioress and, in general, enforcing masculine control over the nuns. Ana de Jesús and María de San José, leaders of the "rebel nuns," resisted such modifications and petitioned Pope Sixtus V to forbid changes (without papal approval) to the constitutions. Initially they were successful; the pope complied with their request in a 1590 brief. But in the following year his successor, Gregory XIV, rescinded the brief and approved most of Doria's revisions. In a cruel episode in Carmelite history, Doria retaliated by stripping Ana de Jesús and María de San José of their authority and sentencing them to periods of confinement. As this episode illustrates, women identified as Teresa's heirs held a status that was both exalted and precarious.

Clashes of authority continued as the order spread outside of Spain. As Kavanaugh shows, Ana de San Bartolomé quarreled with her French superior, Pierre de Bérulle, over his interpretation of the rule. She insisted that her intimacy with Teresa trumped his erudition: "I contradicted him, and he said he knew these things quite as well as I. I told him that was not so; that he must be great in book-learning, but that he had no experience, as I did, of matters concerning the Order."[7] Differences in judgment could even bring the nuns into conflict with each other. Ana de Jesús and Ana de San Bartolomé had several flare-ups; they took opposing sides during the nuns' revolt (the latter Ana endorsed the Dorian reforms) and sometimes expressed resentment of each other's sense of ownership of the Founding

Mother's legacy. Their own protégées, in turn, perpetuated the rivalry during the campaigns to secure each Ana's beatification.

As can be seen in the essays, Teresa's heirs struggled to keep pace with a rapidly changing and expanding order. During her lifetime Teresa accomplished the near impossible, successfully negotiating challenges she faced as a woman in a male dominated society, a mystic, a descendant of converted Jews, and the leader of a religious reform that aroused intermittent opposition from civic and ecclesiastical authorities. Her successors faced the problem of holding together her agenda. They were not always successful, since some of the saint's more revolutionary policies were reversed soon her death. In 1587 the Discalced Carmelites began to require a minimum dowry payment from female novices, a policy that María de San José decried as "something very foreign to our Holy Mother."[8] In 1597 the order joined most other Spanish monastic communities by establishing statutes of "purity of blood," which denied entrance to the descendants of *converso*s (converted Jews) extending back four generations. This policy, ironically, would have prevented Teresa herself from joining the order that she founded.[9] When the Discalced Carmelites expanded into France, language barriers, cultural differences, and disparate interpretations of the Teresian constitutions inevitably led to tensions. For example, the wall of separation that Teresa had tried to maintain between lay elite and her nuns eroded, since the aristocratic women who organized and financed French monastic institutions expected regular entrance into the enclosure of the convents they patronized. Though the Spanish nuns feared that the intrusion of lay benefactors inevitably corrupted the enclosed nuns' lives of austerity and constant prayer, they found it impossible to resist these types of visits that brought tangible rewards aiding the order's expansion throughout France. Some of the Spanish Carmelites complained that the French nuns were prone to laxness and needed constant reinforcement in rigorous poverty. When Ana de Jesús, for example, found a feather pillow in the attic of the recently founded Dijon Carmel, she ordered it taken away and given to the poor, telling her companion that "if the French find it here, they will make use of it, and our blessed mother not wanting this, we should not have it."[10] Though Teresa's daughters were sometimes frustrated by what they perceived as the thwarting of her intentions due to political skirmishes or local conditions outside of Spain, such situations nevertheless gave them the opportunity to assert their identities as her legitimate successors.

Despite difficulties and setbacks, Teresa's heirs also experienced important successes. In addition to their energetic foundation of new Discalced Carmelite communities, the individuals discussed here led the effort to publish and disseminate Teresa's written works, beginning with the first edition (Salamanca, 1588) that was spearheaded by Ana de Jesús; they distributed miracle-working relics and commissioned works of art depicting the saint; they forged alliances with key political figures, such as Marie de Medici of France and the Archdukes Albert and Isabella of the Spanish Netherlands; and they pushed forward the process of Teresa's beatification (1614) and canonization (1622). Motivated by love for the foundress, Teresa's heirs strove to carry out her will a resolute determination—*muy determinada determinación*, as the saint puts it in *The Way of Perfection* (21.2) —and to extend her reputation for sanctity throughout the world.

I join my two symposium co-organizers, Barbara Mujica and Alison Weber, in expressing deep gratitude to the Institute of Carmelite Studies, the Carmelitana Collection of Whitefriars Hall, and Georgetown University's Department of Spanish and Portuguese for their generosity in sponsoring this event; to John Sullivan, O.C.D., Steven Payne, O.C.D., and Patrick McMahon,

O.Carm., for their enthusiastic guidance and support; to the scholars who contributed papers and to all those who attended. It is our hope that these papers will stimulate further interest in the extraordinarily rich Teresian legacy.

Christopher C. Wilson

---

1   Teresa of Ávila, *The Way of Perfection,* 1.2, in *The Collected Works of St. Teresa of Ávila,* trans. Kieran Kavanaugh, O.C.D., and Otilio Rodríguez, O.C.D., 3 vols. (Washington, D.C.: Institute of Carmelite Studies Publications, 1976-85).

2   Ana de San Bartolomé, "Origenes del Carmelo Teresiano en Francia," in *Obras completas de la Beata Ana de San Bartolomé,* ed. Julián Urkiza, O.C.D., 2 vols. (Rome: Teresianum, 1985), 1:172 (cited hereafter as OCASB), quoted in translation in *Autobiography of the Blessed Mother Anne of Saint Bartholomew,* trans. by a religious of the Carmel of St. Louis (St. Louis, 1916), 48.

3   Barbara Diefendorf, *From Penitence to Charity: Pious Women and the Catholic Reformation in Paris* (New York: Oxford University Press, 2004), 116.

4   For Teresa's concern with the spiritual welfare of Native Americans, see chapter 1 of *The Book of Her Foundations.*

5   See OCASB; Ildefonso Moriones, O.C.D., *Ana de Jesús y la herencia teresiana: Humanismo cristiano o rigor primitivo?* (Rome: Teresianum, 1968); *Just Man, Husband of Mary, Guardian of Christ: An Anthology of Readings from Jerónimo Gracián's Summary of the Excellencies of St. Joseph (1597),* ed. and trans. Joseph F. Chorpenning, O.S.F.S. (Philadelphia: Saint Joseph's University Press, 1993); Ana de San Agustín, *The Visionary Life of Madre Ana de San Agustín,* ed. Elizabeth Teresa Howe (Suffolk, England: Tamesis Press, 2004); Electa Arenal and Stacey Schlau, *Untold Sisters: Hispanic Nuns in Their Own Works,* with translations by Amanda Powell (Albuquerque: University of New Mexico Press, 1989); Barbara Mujica, *Women Writers of*

Early Modern Spain: Sophia's Daughters (New Haven and London: Yale University Press, 2004); María de San José Salazar, *Book for the Hour of Recreation,* introduction and notes by Alison Weber, trans. Amanda Powell (Chicago and London: University of Chicago Press, 2002).

6   Elisabeth Stopp, "Spanish Links: St. Francis de Sales and St. Teresa of Ávila," in *A Man to Heal Differences: Essays and Talks on St. Francis de Sales* (Philadelphia: Saint Joseph's University Press, 1997), 171-82, at 173; Saint Francis de Sales, Preface to *The Love of God: A Treatise,* trans. Vincent Kerns (Westminster, MD: Newman Press, 1962), 27-40, at 29.

7   Ana de San Bartolomé, *Autobiografía A,* in OCASB, 1:348-49, quoted in translation in Arenal and Schlau, 64.

8   Jodi Bilinkoff, "Teresa of Jesus and the Carmelite Reform," in *Religious Orders of the Catholic Reformation* (New York: Fordham University Press, 1994), 165-86, at 177.

9   Bilinkoff, 177.

10   Diefendorf, 108.

María de San José (Salazar): Saint Teresa's "Difficult" Daughter

Alison Weber
University of Virginia

"Difficult" is one of those words that, at least in contemporary American English, is "gender inflected"—it takes on different connotations according to the sex of the person described. What do we mean when we say that a *woman* is "difficult?" Chances are we mean she has a forceful personality and strong opinions, characteristics that would be considered assets for a man but handicaps for a woman. Among the many talented women who formed the first generation of Saint Teresa's heirs, María de San José Salazar (1548-1603) stands out as one of the most "difficult." Her strong personality and penchant for independent decision-making brought her into conflict on a number of occasions with the mother foundress, with the nuns in her charge, and with her prelates. This intelligent and cultivated woman, whom Teresa loved and admired enough to imagine as her successor, ended her days in disgrace in the eyes of her monastic superiors.

María may have been difficult, but she was also a true and loyal daughter of Saint Teresa. She understood aspects of Teresa's spirituality and the goals of the reform perhaps better than any other nun in the first Discalced generation. Yet she found herself on the losing side of an internecine struggle over the meaning of the Teresian legacy. How could this happen? I want to make clear at the outset that my intention in describing María as "difficult" is not to blame María for her misfortunes but rather to try to understand something of the interplay of circumstance and individual identity in shaping the early history of the reform. Historians, with reason, are reluctant to write about the influ-

1

ence of character on historical events; it is too easy, after all, to fall into the trap of anachronistic psychologizing or romantic invention. I would argue, however, that if our goal is to understand historical movements and organizations, it is useful to try to reconstruct the interpersonal dynamics of their leaders and their disciples.

Such histories, of course, will always be tentative. Even when we have a good cache of primary sources, the process of piecing together divergent viewpoints involves a fair amount of speculation and interpretation. In the case of María de San José, we are relatively fortunate in our sources: we have the sixty-four letters Teresa wrote to María between 1576 and 1582, Teresa's *Book of Foundations,* María's autobiographical histories of the reform, *Libro de recreaciones (Book for the Hour of Recreation)* and *Ramillete de mirra (Bough of Myrrh),* and various legal documents. Other key documents have disappeared, however, including María's letters to Teresa. Nevertheless, I believe it is possible to recover some sense of the interpersonal dynamics at work in this particularly sad chapter in Carmelite history.

The first of the many enigmas surrounding this Carmelite nun has to do with her origins. The Spanish scholar María Pilar Manero Sorolla, after extensive research in different convent archives, has uncovered the following. The *Book of Professions* from Malagón, where María made her profession, states that she was known in the world as María de Salazar and that she was the daughter of Pedro de Velasco and María de Salazar, natives of Aragón. But the records from the convent of San José in Seville, where María was later prioress, affirm that she was a native of Toledo and the daughter of Sebastián de Salazar and Doña María de Torre. None of these personas has been identified. A seventeenth-century Portuguese historian of the Discalced Carmelites records that she was a distant relative of the dukes of Medinaceli. Manero Sorolla speculates that María was not a distant relative but the illegitimate daughter of Gastón de la Cerda, the third duke of Medinaceli.[1] Whatever her connection to the family, María was raised with solicitous care by the duke's sister, Doña Luisa de la Cerda. Doña Luisa was one of the richest noblewomen of Castile. She and her husband belonged to the highest rank of aristocrats: the *grandes*. In Doña Luisa's magnificent palace in Toledo, María received an extraordinary education for a woman of her day. She studied French and Latin and became a skilled poet in Spanish. As a member of Doña Luisa's court, María would have known the Princess Juana of Austria, the Marquises of Villena and Ávila, and Doña Luisa's cousin, Ana de Mendoza, the princess of Eboli.

Despite her great wealth and power, Doña Luisa was also very pious. Theologians, religious reformers, and figures renowned for their holiness were invited to her palace. When Doña Luisa's husband died in 1562, the grieving widow sought out the companionship of a Carmelite nun from Ávila, Doña Teresa de Ahumada, as she was known at the time. María, then just twelve years old, describes the impact of this visit:

> "[What impressed me] was the gentleness and prudence of our good Mother. In truth I believe that if those whose work it is to bring souls to God were to use the same schemes and skill that were used by this saint, many more women would come to religious life than are coming now...."[2]

Meanwhile, Teresa's friendship with Doña Luisa continued to grow, and in 1568 the noblewoman provided Teresa with an endowment for her third foundation in Malagón, a town that formed part of her feudal estates. María took the habit there in 1570 and in 1572, at the age of twenty-four, she was elected prioress. Had Doña Luisa endowed Malagón to provide a suitable position for her protégée, someone whose marriage prospects may well have been limited? It is not necessary to impugn the piety of either woman to see that "placing" María may have figured in the constellation of Doña Luisa's motives. Traditionally, monastic patronage came with strings attached, and a priorate for María may have been part of the unspoken bargain between the noblewoman and the foundress. Fortunately for Teresa, María was highly capable. Fortunately for María, Teresa's gentle but purposeful vision of religious life provided an attractive alternative to a comfortable but banal existence in an aristocratic convent.[3] María, by her own account, willingly embraced her decision to spend her life in austere circumstances among women from the middling urban classes. But it is also evident that having done so, she expected to be in charge.

In 1575 Teresa chose María to accompany her in establishing new convents in Beas, Caravaca, and Seville. The first two foundations went relatively smoothly, but the third was beset with so many difficulties that Teresa later referred to her time in the southern metropolis as *"el infierno de Sevilla"*—the hell of Seville. Despite assurances to the contrary, the archbishop offered no support, the Franciscans were openly hostile, and the expected alms from wealthy *Sevillanos* failed to materialize. María describes their lukewarm welcome in Seville:

> We entered ... the twenty-sixth of May [1575] .... Father Mariano had rented a house for us, quite small and damp, on the Calle de las Armas, where two ladies who were his friends received us. That day they accompanied us there and then they left, and for a very long time we saw nothing more of them, nor

did they or anyone else send us so much as a jug of water. ….
Let us relate in detail the furniture and effects we found in that
house. First were half a dozen old cane-stalk frames that Father
Mariano had ordered; … these lay on the floor to be used as
beds. There were two or three very dirty little mattresses, like
those of Discalced friars, and accompanied by a crowd of such
creatures as usually do accompany them [i.e., fleas].[4]

This initial distress was alleviated when Teresa's brother
Lorenzo de Cepeda returned from the New World and provided most
of the money for the purchase of a new house. A local priest by the
name of Garciálvarez offered invaluable assistance in these early
days. Teresa was enormously grateful to him and was delighted when
he became the first chaplain and confessor at San José.

The trials in Seville were just beginning, however. In December
of 1575 a disaffected novice named María del Corro denounced
Teresa and her nuns to the Inquisition. She charged, among other
things, that the nuns prayed with their faces to the wall (a Jewish practice) after receiving communion. The nuns admitted that this was true,
but explained that since they did not have enough veils, a nun who had
made her confession would pass her veil on to the next sister in line,
and then face the wall in the patio to avoid the glare of the Andalusian
sun. The Inquisition initiated an investigation and, finding the allegations groundless, did not proceed further.[5]

Meanwhile, conflict within the order was reaching crisis propor-
tions. Many felt that Jerónimo Gracián, Teresa's beloved confessor,
had overstepped his authority as visitator in Andalusia. It was
revealed, furthermore, that he had lacked jurisdictional authority when
he ordered Teresa to make a foundation in Andalusia. (The Carmelite
General, Juan Bautista Rubeo, had given her patents to found only in

Castile). In 1576, Rubeo turned against the Discalced and ordered Teresa to return to Castile and desist from further foundational efforts. María, just twenty-seven years old herself, was left to preside over an inexperienced and already traumatized community. She and the nuns in her charge, to make matters worse, suffered from periodic fevers, possibly caused by malaria.

Shortly after Teresa's departure two nuns, Isabel de San Jerónimo and Beatriz de la Madre de Dios (Chávez), began to report receiving visions and hearing voices in prayer. Were these spiritually gifted or spiritually troubled nuns? Were their experiences divine gifts or products of a sick imagination? We know from Teresa's writings that she had developed a very practical method for dealing with reports of visions, locutions, and similar phenomena, and that she expected prioresses to regularly monitor and guide their nuns' spiritual progress. Indeed, the constitutions stipulated that "all the sisters should give the prioress a monthly account of how they have done in prayer."[6] Teresa's first guideline for prioresses was to rule out a physical cause. Demonstrating her familiarity with the medical theories of her day, Teresa believed that an imbalance in the body's four humors, brought on by insufficient food and sleep, could cause noxious humors to rise from the stomach to the brain, thereby producing delusions. Therefore, she urged prioresses to make sure that their subordinates did not engage in "indiscrete" penitential practices. Her second principle was to avoid lavishing attention on such nuns. This was based on her suspicion that reported graces were sometimes nothing more than a bid for attention. Third, Teresa advised her prioresses to consult with learned theologians experienced in prayer—if they were available. Otherwise, they should maintain a discrete silence until the situation became clearer. Above all Teresa counseled, time and again, that prioresses should not rush to judgment but rather wait patiently, for true favors will be known by their good effects within the community over time.[7] This is precisely what Teresa recommended for the problematic Seville nuns. In a letter dated 23 October 1576, Teresa writes Jerónimo Gracián, who apparently was consulting frequently with María:

> It will be necessary to make [Isabel de] San Jerónimo eat meat for a few days and give up prayer, and tell her not to speak to anyone but you, or that she write to me, for her imagination is weak and what she meditates on she thinks she sees or hears. Sometimes, though, what she says will be true and has been, for she is a very good soul. And I think that the same goes for Beatriz....She, too, should fast only sparingly.[8]

Four months later, Isabel de San Jerónimo was recovering in another convent, but Beatriz continued to report supernatural experiences: "In regard to Beatriz, her prayer is good, but insofar as possible avoid paying attention to these things in conversations or any other way. You know this depends very much on the prioress."[9]

Throughout the spring and summer of 1578, Teresa offered advice to the Seville prioress about how to deal with Beatriz and a lay sister, Margarita de la Concepción:

> Before I forget: I do not approve of your nuns' writing on subjects to do with prayer; there are many disadvantages in the practice. . . .You must realize that it is not only a waste of time; it interferes with the soul's freedom of action, and then, too, it may lead the nuns to imagine all kinds of things. If I remember, I will say this to our Farther [Gracián]; if I do not, you should speak to him about it yourself. If their experiences are of any

substance, they will never forget them; and if they are of a kind that can be forgotten, there is no point in their writing them down.... If I had appeared to attach any importance to the things [Isabel de] San Jerónimo told me, she would never have stopped....[10]

A few months later, Teresa writes:

I was extremely glad to hear that our Father [Gracián] is telling those two nuns who are so much given to prayer that they must eat meat. You know, my daughter, I have been worried about them: they would not have had such a whirl of experiences if they had been with me. The very fact that they have so many of these experiences makes me suspicious about them, and, though some of them may be genuine, I am sure it will be best if they regard them as of little importance, and if your Reverence and our Father do the same, or indeed treat them as of no account at all, for nothing will be lost by that even if they are genuine.[11]

From this letter it is clear that María has been working closely with Gracián and that both have followed Teresa's first principle of improved diet to rule out a "humoral" (today we would say physiological) origin for the experiences. Yet Teresa obviously suspects that they are still making too much fuss over the situation. We see that María and/or Gracián have ordered the nuns to record their visions in writing, much as Teresa's early confessors had done, as part of a spiritual examination process. We also see that Teresa deemed this exercise unnecessary and possibly harmful. We can appreciate Teresa's apprehensions. These were dark days for the reform. At the time

Teresa was writing, the Calced held John of the Cross imprisoned in Toledo. The new papal nuncio, Felipe Sega, was on the verge of excommunicating Gracián and two other Discalced friars. Malicious rumors about Gracián's over-familiarity with the nuns of Paterna had been circulating. In addition, the Inquisition was concerned over new "outbreaks" of an antinomian heresy called *alumbradismo*. In an *auto de fe* held in Seville on 10 February 1577, three women were punished as *alumbradas*, and in the neighboring province of Extremadura the Inquisition was wrapping up its investigations of a group of visionary *beatas* (lay "holy women") and their confessors.[12] Finally, Teresa's *Life* had been sequestered by the Inquisition. What if Beatriz's and Margarita's visionary writings should fall into the wrong hands? Would this further implicate the Discalced in the hunt for *alumbrados*?

To make matters worse, Garciálvarez, the convent's chaplain and principal confessor, was meeting with Beatriz and Margarita frequently for lengthy general confessions. We do not know whether he considered them "potential" saints or unfortunate victims of demonic obsession.[13] We do know that he and María came to an impasse over who had authority to deal with the situation. Garciálvarez believed that María was trespassing into priestly territory during the monthly "accounts of prayer," and María believed that she had the authority to restrict Garciálvarez's access to the nuns. But when she sought Teresa's support to dismiss Garciálvarez, the mother foundress could not believe that the priest was disrupting the convent to the extent María claimed. From the distance of Castile, she struggled to transmit her philosophy of tolerance, cooperation, and what I call for lack of a better expression "charismatic non-alarmism." In her letters to María, Teresa seldom fails to send warm regards to Garciálvarez, almost as if she hoped that her affection for the chaplain would rub off on the prioress.

There were other factors that may have deterred Teresa from taking María's side in this dispute. By the end of 1577, it was evident that María had become quite independent. María was convinced that the house in Seville was unhealthy, and she had begun to make plans to buy a different one—without consulting Teresa! The mother foundress was displeased. As she wrote to María on 10 December 1577, "I can't figure out how you are going to get the money to buy another house, for I don't even remember if the one you are in is paid for.... If you have so much money, don't forget what you owe my brother. He is paying five hundred ducats interest on a property he bought."[14]

Whether from fear of scandal, displeasure with María's intractability, gratitude to an old benefactor, or some combination of the three, Teresa refused to intervene on María's side. In September 1578, she wrote the Seville prioress:

> For the love of Our Lord, daughter, I beg you to suffer and be silent. None of you must try to get that Father [i.e., Garciálvarez] turned out, however many trials and annoyances he may cause you, for they are not so serious as to offend God, and I cannot bear our being ungrateful to anyone who has been good to us.... I have always thought him a servant of God and a well-meaning man. I fully realize that this gratitude of mine is not in the least a sign of perfection: it must be my nature—I could be suborned with a sardine.[15]

Let us consider María's version of events as she relates them in *Book for the Hour of Recreation:*

> At this time our Mother was no longer in Seville. It had been more than two years since she had gone, leaving us a confessor who, though he was a servant of God, was ignorant and confused, with-

out learning or experience. The devil had at that time provided this priest with yet another pious woman for his own aims; this caused me to try *to take him in hand* in certain matters in which he was interfering and some singular practices he took up with two Sisters finding excuses to stay with them from morning until night....These confessions lasted some three or four months. When I wished to put an end to such excess, he went to all Seville to ask whether they thought that the Prioress could interfere in confessions.... He was upsetting everything and bringing the house down about my ears, freeing the nuns from their obedience. Finding myself in this state, I informed our Mother so that she could solve the problem. She told me I should endure him and dissemble, for it was not the right time to do anything more, since God had given the devil permission to torment and afflict us. (my emphasis)[16]

María did not accept Teresa's advice to put up with Garciálvarez but rather proceeded to "take him in hand." He retaliated by denouncing the convent to the Calced fathers. Due to an unfortunate turn of events, the Discalced in Seville were now under the jurisdiction of the Fathers of the Observance. The provincial, Diego de Cárdenas, came down hard on the nuns of San José and initiated an official visitation during which the nuns, threatened and intimidated, confessed to a bizarre conglomeration of heretical and moral offenses. One accusation, for example, declared that the nuns were forced to make sacramental confessions to their prioresses.[17] María records the following in her autobiographical narrative, *Bough of Myrrh*:

[They] put together lies that they had already invented about Father Gracián and other Discalced nuns, especially our saintly

mother…with the most abominable and dirtiest words that can
be imagined….The least offensive thing that can be said…was
that that wicked old lady [i.e., Teresa], with the excuse of founding convents, took women from one place to another so that
they might be wicked [i.e., to found houses of prostitution]. And
what our saintly mother answered when she read this was, "As
long as they are going to lie, it's better that they lie in such a way
that no one believes them, and laugh about it."[18]

In the wake of the scandal, María was removed from office at
the end of 1578, deprived of voice and vote, and sentenced to confinement in her cell for six months. To her further humiliation, Beatriz was
appointed interim prioress. Although Cárdenas submitted memoranda
to the Inquisition, there is no evidence that the Holy Office followed
up on the case.[19] Within a year the balance of power had shifted, in part
due to efforts by the king and the nuncio to restore peace within the
order. In 1579, Garciálvarez was banned from the convent and the
new vicar-general, Angel de Salazar, restored María's privileges. The
nuns eventually retracted their accusations.[20]

Teresa had been distressed over her inability to head off the crisis in Seville and had worked behind the scenes to bring about María's
reinstatement.[21] But what to do in the aftermath of the crisis? In a
remarkable letter to the Seville convent dated 3 May 1579, Teresa
details her recommendations for this difficult period of readjustment:

I loved you all dearly as it was, but I love you twice as much
now, especially your Reverence [María] who has been the chief
sufferer…. Although I know my daughter Josefa is very wicked,
I know, too, that she fears God, and would never have committed any sin against His Majesty which could merit such a pun-

ishment. . . . I am sorry Garciálvarez is not saying Mass for you now….We are certainly indebted to him…. In some ways I look upon [Beatriz] as a person out of her mind. You see, I know of certain persons…whose imagination is so unstable that they think they really see everything that comes into their minds. The devil must be at the back of this. The first thing I want to say is that you must commend [Beatriz] to His Majesty very earnestly in all your prayers—pray for her every moment of the day, if you can….Your love for God, my sisters, must show itself in your pity for her which must be as great as though she were as much the daughter of your father as she is of this our true Father…. *Try to forget what has happened,* and think, each of you, how you would like to be treated if it had happened to you. (my emphasis)[22]

Teresa closes the letter sending warm regards to Garciálvarez and adds this curious remembrance for Beatriz: "Remember me to Sister Beatriz de la Madre de Dios, and tell her how glad I am she now has no work, for in a letter she wrote me she said how much work that office gave her."[23]

There is no question about the central message here—forgiveness all around. But the letter is laced with irony. As sociolinguists have shown, irony has multiple and sometimes contradictory functions. It can be used to reinforce solidarity, as if the speaker or writer were saying, "we know each other so well and are such good friends that we can play language games and still understand each other." But irony, like any kind of teasing, can also have a sting. Is Teresa really glad that Beatriz no longer has so much work to do as ex-prioress? Or is this a subtle reminder to the nun that she was eminently unsuited for the task? How are we to interpret "I know my daughter Josefa is very wicked"?[24] Surely this is primarily an example of ironic antithesis—saying the opposite of what one means. Teresa knows María is not "very wicked" but very good, and that she has suffered unjustly. (Note that Teresa rarely used affectionate nicknames with her prioresses; here, "Josefa" must also count as an endearment.) But why use humor at all in these sad circumstances? Perhaps this was Teresa's way of giving María a lesson in humility, and perhaps a way of getting her attention. As sympathetic as she may have been for María's suffering, Teresa needed to let her know that this was not the time for recrimination, retaliation, and self-pity, but for spiritual amnesty. If a little grim humor helped get the message across, so much the better.[25]

Teresa was delighted when the new vicar-general reinstated María as prioress on 12 July 1579. "That news has given me the greatest comfort, for no other solution could have brought souls tranquility."[26] But María's resistance to Teresa's style of micro-management was a continual source of friction. There was the matter of the debt to Teresa's brother Lorenzo, which María, despite repeated urgings, failed to pay off.[27] Teresa was particularly annoyed that María continued to look for a new house. As Teresa wrote to Gracián, "I find [mischief] in that house which is intolerable, and the prioress is shrewder than befits her vocation…. To keep telling the poor nuns how bad the house is for them is enough to put the idea into their heads that they are ill. I have written her some terrible letters, but you might as well talk to a stone wall."[28] When Don Lorenzo died in June of 1580, his will stipulated that the 430 *ducados* the convent owed him should go toward the construction of his funeral chapel in St. Joseph's of Ávila. Over the next twenty months, Teresa wrote at least six letters in which she repeatedly begged María to repay the loan.[29] We have no way of knowing why María dragged her heels in this matter.

Although María clearly exasperated Teresa at times, the

foundress had deep reserves of affection and esteem for the Seville prioress, as we can see from this letter, written shortly before her death:

> I was amused to know what prestige your belfry has brought you: [if it has such a fine bell] as you say it is fully justified.… You express yourself so well that, if my opinion were acted upon, they would elect you Foundress after my death; indeed, I should be very pleased it they did so during my lifetime, as you know so much more, and are so much better, than I.[30]

María did not become Teresa's successor, but she did lead an important foundation in Lisbon in 1584. More difficult days were ahead, however. Her close friendship with Gracián drew her into his bitter struggle with his successor, Nicolás Doria. Doria was convinced that the reform was sliding into laxity and wanted to restructure the order's system of governance, placing the nuns firmly under the authority of the friars. Like Gracián, María opposed Doria's rigorism, and with Ana de Jesús she led a "nuns' rebellion" against Doria's plans to change Teresa's constitutions.[31] In 1593 Doria removed María from office and imprisoned her incommunicado for nine months. Ten years later, for reasons that to this day are obscure, María was transferred to the isolated convent of Cuerva, where she died on 19 October 1603. Almost four hundred years later, in 1999, the general definitory of the Discalced Carmelites expressed great regret for the severe punishment that had been imposed on her and on Ana de Jesús.

What is the point of rehearsing these painful events? As I suggested at the beginning of this paper, examining Teresa's relationship with her "difficult" daughter can give us insight into the more general difficulties Teresa faced in perpetuating the spirit of religious renewal. First, we can understand the drag of traditional interests and ways of thinking. Negotiating the competing interests of patrons and clients, members of the aristocracy and the new urban middling class, and prioresses and prelates required extraordinary diplomatic skills, which Teresa possessed in abundance. María, illegitimate or not, belonged to a much higher social stratum than Teresa and most of the other Discalced nuns and friars with whom she had to deal. Obedience did not come as easily for such a woman as did "taking people in hand." Second, Teresa's non-alarmist, "wait-and-see" approach to discerning supernatural favors was difficult to teach. None of the parties involved—María, Gracián, and Garciálvarez—seemed able to follow Teresa's advice in full. Finally, the relative autonomy that Teresa had given prioresses as spiritual leaders of their convents went against the grain of a patriarchal church. María's failure when she tried to take Garciálvarez "in hand" is less surprising than Teresa's many successes in winning over hostile prelates.

This paper has emphasized the Teresian lessons that María, as a twenty-something prioress in Seville, could not appreciate: patience, tolerance for the weakness of others, and the importance of persuasive courtesy. But her writings reveal that there was much, much more that she did capture. *Book for the Hour of Recreation,* written in 1585, synthesizes and endorses Teresa's philosophy of *"suavedad"* or gentleness, moderation in penance, and non-alarmism in questions of discernment. María also grasped Teresa's Christian feminism, her belief that women could be apostles, if not preachers, and serve the church by "bringing souls to God." Her spirited defense of the Teresian constitutions was motivated by her conviction that they preserved Teresa's wish that nuns have access to the best spiritual advice available.[32] It is poignantly ironic that in María's declaration for Teresa's beatification process, she testifies at length on Teresa's prudence and diplomacy: "She was always firm and constant in what seemed to her the service of our Lord; and in everything she achieved what she attempted, but in such a way that the parties involved ended up in peace and concord, although they often had pursued the opposite of what Mother Teresa was attempting."[33] And in a guidebooks for prioresses written when she was forty-two, María gives indications that she had come to appreciate yet another Teresian lesson:

> The prioresses should not think that they must always be giving orders, for it is very good for them to persuade and beseech in a gentle and sisterly fashion…. Ponder a great deal on what your saintly mother Teresa de Jesús put in the Constitutions: the prioress should try to be loved so that she may be obeyed. This is my first piece of advice: let her win the hearts of her subordinates with love, . . . so that she may govern them with greater peace and profit.[34]

[1] María Pilar Manero Sorolla, "On the Margins of the Mendozas: Luisa de la Cerda and María de San José (Salazar)," in *Power and Gender in Renaissance Spain: Eight Women of the Mendoza Family,* 1450-1650, ed. Helen Nader (Urbana: University of Illinois Press, 2004), 113-31, at 114.

[2] María de San José Salazar, *Book for the Hour of Recreation,* introduction and notes by Alison Weber and trans. Amanda Powell (Chicago: University of Chicago Press, 2002), 45.

[3] On Teresa's reform as a purposeful "mission" for cloistered women, see Jodi Bilinkoff, *The Ávila of Saint Teresa* (Ithaca: Cornell University Press, 1989). As can be seen from María's words cited above, she conceived of her vocation in terms of a mission to "bring souls to God."

[4] She continues, "That house was well set up indeed for the heat to afflict us. Many days our dinner was nothing but apples and bread, sometimes cooked up and sometimes in salad, and there were days when there was nothing but one loaf of bread" (*Book for the Hour of Recreation,* 146).

[5] On the Seville denunciations, see Enrique Llamas Martínez, *Santa Teresa de*

Jesús y la Inquisición española (Madrid: CSIC, 1972), 53-194, and Gillian T.W. Ahlgren, *Teresa of Ávila and the Politics of Sanctity* (Ithaca: Cornell University Press, 1996), 52-61.

[6]   *The Constitutions,* in *The Collected Works of St. Teresa of Ávila,* trans. Kieran Kavanaugh, O.C.D., and Otilio Rodríguez, O.C.D., 3 vols. (Washington, D.C.: ICS Publications, 1976-85), 3:331.

[7]   I discuss Teresa's practice of discernment in "Spiritual Administration: Gender and Discernment in the Carmelite Reform," *Sixteenth Century Journal* 31 (2000): 123-46.

[8]   *The Collected Letters of St. Teresa of Ávila,* trans. Kieran Kavanaugh, O.C.D. (Washington, D.C.: ICS Publications, 2001), 1:370. This volume contains letters written through December, 1577. Volume 2 is forthcoming. When possible, I will cite this edition, hereafter abbreviated as Kavanaugh. I have also consulted the Spanish edition, *Epistolario de Santa Teresa de Jesús,* ed. Luis Rodríguez Martínez and Teófanes Egido, 2nd ed. (Madrid: Espiritualidad, 1984).

[9]   1-2 March 1577, in Kavanaugh, 1:516. I discuss Teresa's attempts to educate María in the discernment of spirits in greater detail in "Dear Daughter: Reform and Persuasion in Saint Teresa's Letters to her Prioresses," in *Form and Persuasion in Women's Informal Letters. 1500-1700,* ed. Ann Crabb and Jane Couchman (Aldershot: Ashgate, 2005), 241-61.

[10]   28 March 1578, in *The Letters of Saint Teresa of Jesus,* ed. E. Allison Peers, 2 vols. (Westminster, MD: Newman Press, 1959), 2:544. For letters written after 1577, I refer to this edition.

[11]   4 June1578, in Peers, *Letters,* 2:575.

[12]   Ahlgren, 58. *Alumbradismo* or Illuminism was a catch-all term for a variety of heretical, novel, or enthusiastic religious beliefs and behaviors. On the Extremaduran Alumbrados see Alison Weber, "Demonizing Ecstasy: Alonso de la Fuente and the *Alumbrados* of Extremadura," in *The Mystical Gesture: Medieval and Early Modern Spiritual Culture in Honor of Mary E. Giles,* ed. Robert Boenig (Aldershot: Ashgate, 2000), 147-165. E. Allison Peers' *Handbook to the Life and Times of St. Teresa and St. John of the Cross* (London: Burns and Oates, 1954) contains a useful biographical and historical outline of these disputes.

[13]   At this time many believed that the devil tormented or tempted persons who were especially virtuous or who were making spiritual progress. These victims

of demonic "obsession" were deemed worthy of solicitous concern.

[14] Kavanaugh, 1:589-90.

[15] Peers, *Letters,* 2:602.

[16] *Book for the Hour of Recreation,* 153.

[17] This was, apparently, Garciálvarez's interpretation of what happened in the monthly "accounts of prayer."

[18] María de San José, *Ramillete de mirra* in *Escritos espirituales,* ed. Simeón de la Sagrada Familia (Rome: Postulación General O.C.D., 1979), 303 (my translation).

[19] As María writes in *Ramillete de mirra,* "In the end, as the accusations were like what the other nun [María de Corro] had said, and since they [the Inquisition] had already investigated, they didn't pay any attention to them" (305, my translation). This is not surprising. The Inquisitors had a healthy respect for monastic jurisdiction and concentrated their attention on allegations against the behavior and beliefs of *beatas,* or lower class lay holy women. Ahlgren points out that Teresa's superior theological sophistication, her social class, and her political connections also played a role in protecting her from the Inquisition (*Teresa of Ávila and the Politics of Sanctity*, 60-61).

[20] Some time around 1580 Beatriz turned against Garciálvarez. Teresa continued to defend him, insisting that Beatriz was the one who had made him act foolishly. See the letter to María de San José, 4 July 1580 (Peers, *Letters,* 2:760). The accusations submitted to the Inquisition have not been found. Llamas reproduces the texts of the nuns' retractions in *Santa Teresa . . . Inquisición,* 195-219.

[21] See letter of April, 1579 to Gracián. Salazar shortly thereafter removed Beatriz from office and appointed Isabel de San Jerónimo as interim prioress.

[22] Peers, *Letters,* 2:646-49.

[23] Peers, *Letters,* 2:645-53.

[24] Peers' translation of *harto ruin* as "very wicked" sounds especially harsh to American ears; "very naughty" is perhaps a closer equivalent to contemporary American English.

[25] In a letter dated early January, 1580, Teresa rebukes María more sharply for mishandling the incident: "I was amazed at some of the things your Reverence wrote, and at the notice you took of the sisters. Where had your common sense got to?" (Peers, *Letters,* 2:707). Teresa did support María's efforts to have Beatriz retract her charges. When Beatriz proved recalcitrant, Teresa agreed

with María's decision to punish her with confinement. See the letter to María de San José dated 4 July 1580, in Peers, *Letters,* 2:758.

[26] Peers, *Letters,* 2:674. Peers notes that although Salazar's patent reinstating María was issued on 28 June 1579, María was reluctant to return to office and did not assume this position until 12 July (2:674, note 2).

[27] See, for example, the letters of 22 July 1579; early January, 1580; 1 February 1580; 8-9 February 1580.

[28] To Jerónimo Gracián, 4 October 1579, in Peers, *Letters,* 2:685. Peers renders *rapacería* as "puerility," for which I have suggested "mischief." See also the letter to María de San José dated early January, 1580 (Peers, *Letters,* 2:705), in which Teresa complains that María has failed to pay heed to her financial advice.

[29] See letters to María dated 6 August 1580; 21 November 1580; 28 December 1580; 8 November 1581; 28 November 1581; and 6 February1582.

[30] 17 March 1582 (Peers, *Letters,* 2:923).

[31] Doria intended, among other things, to prohibit the nuns from choosing confessors outside the order. María's account of the nuns' rebellion is recorded in *Ramillete de mirra.* María and the other participants in the nuns' rebellion vigorously protested Doria's plans to limit the nuns' freedom to choose confessors outside the order.

[32] On María's Christian feminism, see Ildefonso Moriones, *Ana de Jesús y la herencia teresiana* (Rome: Teresianum, 1968), especially 119-24, and my introduction to *Book for the Hour of Recreation,* especially 23-26.

[33] "Declaración en el Proceso de S. Teresa," in *Escritos espirituales,* 349-50 (my translation).

[34] "Consejos que da una priora a otra que ella había criado" (1590) in *Aviso para el gobierno de las religiosas,* ed. José Luis Astigarraga (Rome: Instituto Histórico Teresiano, 1977), 37.

Paul the Enchanter: Saint Teresa's Vow of Obedience to Gracián

Barbara Mujica
Georgetown University

Saint Teresa met Fray Jerónimo Gracián de la Madre de Dios (1545-1614) in the spring of 1575 in Beas, where she had gone to found a convent. He had professed as a Discalced Carmelite friar two years earlier, on 25 April 1573, and was already serving as Carmelite visitator in Andalusia *in solidum* with Francisco Vargas.[1] He was thirty; she was sixty. Teresa was immediately taken with him. She was impressed by his profound spirituality, his charismatic personality, his gentleness, and his solid ideas on governance. They spoke at length on matters concerning the order and found they shared the notion that kindness and sensitivity were more effective tools for guiding souls than severity.

With the exception of John of the Cross, Teresa had not found effective friars for her projects, and Fray Jerónimo seemed an ideal collaborator. Soon after the meeting she wrote to her good friend, Isabel de Santo Domingo, from Beas on 12 May 1575: "Our padre Gracián has been here for over twenty days. I tell you that though I have spoken with him a great deal, I have not yet come to fully grasp the worth of this man. He is without fault in my eyes... I have never seen perfection with so much gentleness."[2]

Teresa often refers to Gracián in hyperbolic terms from 1575 to 1578, perhaps the most difficult years in Carmelite history. She writes to Father Giovanni Battista Rossi (hereafter referred to by his Spanish name, Juan Bautista Rubeo), the Carmelite General, that "Gracián is like an angel" (18 July1575) and tells Bishop Álvaro de Mendoza that he has "such good qualities" (11 May 1575).[3] Her affection is evident in a letter she wrote to him on 7 December 1576, in which she uses the code name "Paul" for Gracián: "I hope in God that everything will go well, for the Lord is turning Paul into an enchanter."[4] When María de San José, Prioress of the Seville Carmel, fell ill that same month, Teresa wrote to her, "I don't know how you can be sick since you have our padre [Gracián] there" (13 December 1576).[5] Mary Luti, who has studied the relationship between the two, concludes that Teresa was, quite simply, "enthralled."[6]

Some historians and biographers have depicted Teresa as positively giddy upon meeting Gracián, commenting on the "womanliness" of her reaction. Marcelle Auclair, a French biographer writing in the 1940s, comments: "Teresa of Jesus was so excited that she almost seemed like Doña Teresa de Ahumada again."[7] E. Allison Peers writes that "the effect which the charm and apparent saintliness of this young man had on the woman of nearly sixty was almost incredible... she could not put Fray Jerónimo out of her thoughts."[8] Joachim Smet notes: "It is an interesting insight into the femininity of St. Teresa that this personable, intelligent but imprudent young man should have so completely captivated her."[9] José Alberto Pedra comments in his study of Gracián that Teresa was undergoing all kinds of problems at the time she met the young visitator, not the least of which was the Princess of Eboli's denunciation of the *Vida* to the Valladolid Inquisition. "Why," asks Pedra, "would she write, with the enthusiasm of a young girl, that her time in Beas was the happiest in her life? Because that's where she met Father Gracián in person."[10] All of these scholars describe Teresa's meeting with Gracián as something of a thunderbolt.

There can be no doubt but that Teresa was immediately taken with Gracián. She writes in her *Book of Foundations:*

When… Father Maestro Fray Jerónimo Gracián came to see me at Beas, we had never previously met… I was extremely delighted when I learned he was there, for I greatly desired to meet him on account of the good reports given me concerning him. But much greater was my happiness when I began speaking with him, for it seemed from the way he pleased me that those who had praised him had hardly known him at all.[11]

She goes on to explain that the Lord showed her that much good would come to the reform through Gracián. Her interest in him was both spiritual and practical. He was a deeply devout man, filled with zeal for her project, and his approach to convent administration was similar to her own.

For some scholars, Teresa's friendship with Gracián was the most important in her life. In his overview of Teresa's correspondence with her younger disciple, Alfonso Ruiz concludes: "Even if we had no other evidence, (her letters alone) would be enough to show us that the love that united these two people was so profound and unusual that instances of such affection can hardly be found… Gracián displaces, when he appears on the scene, all the other friends who had won a place in the saint's always loving heart, outstripping the competition."[12] A surprising and seemingly impetuous decision by Teresa, made not long after meeting Gracián, would seem to validate this assessment.

In 1575 Teresa decided to make a vow of obedience to Gracián, who, in turn, determined to consult Teresa on all matters concerning the order. Teresa describes this resolution in her *Spiritual Testimonies:*

On the second day of Pentecost, while at Ecija, a person was recalling the great favor she had received from our Lord on the

vigil of this feast. Desiring to do something very special in His
service, she thought it would be good to promise from that time
on not to hide any fault or sin she had committed in her whole
life from the one who stood in God's place... And she also
promised to do all that this confessor might tell her... The first
reason why she decided to do so was the thought that she was
rendering some service to the Holy Spirit; the second was that
she chose a person who was a great servant of God and a
learned man, who would help her serve the Lord more.[13]

Teresa explains that this vow required considerable inner strug-
gle, since it involved a degree of relinquishment of authority.
However, her decision is confirmed by a vision in which God, acting
as a matchmaker, joins her hand to Gracián's: "It seemed to me our
Lord Jesus Christ was next to me... and at his right side stood Master
Gracián himself, and I at His left. The Lord took our right hands and
joined them and told me He desired that I take this master to represent
Him as long as I live."[14]

Teresa says she struggled against this vision because, first,
she feared she would be unable to execute the vow of obedience with
any perfection, and second, she was disinclined to give up her freedom. However, Jesus illuminated her regarding His wish that she put
herself under Gracián's obedience: "And at this point I knelt down and
promised that for the rest of my life I would do everything Master
Gracián might tell me."[15] Rather than enslaving her, she explains, the
vow made her freer because she felt she was better serving God.

Teresa's use of marriage imagery occurs again in a letter to
Gracián written in 1577. Referring to herself by the code name of
Ángela and to Gracián by the code name of Paul, she writes that he
should "be at ease, for the matchmaker was so qualified and made the

knot so tight that it will be taken away only when life ends. And after death the knot will be even tighter, for the foolish striving for perfection will not be so excessive and the remembrance of you will rather help her praise the Lord" (9 January 1577).[16]

The use of the term *casamentero*—matchmaker or marriage broker—and the image of God joining their two hands leaves little doubt that Teresa saw this relationship as a kind of spiritual marriage. But what, exactly, does "spiritual marriage" mean? Some critics have intimated romantic overtones in her use of this image. Luti notes that although "Teresa aspired to objectivity," she is "fairly transparent about the strength of [her] attraction."[17] Auclair suggests that because of her affection for Gracián, Teresa felt "something very much akin to feminine jealousy" for María de San José, the prioress of San José in Seville, with whom Gracián also had a warm friendship.[18]

It is easy to see how biographers could have reached this conclusion. Teresa comments in her *Spiritual Testimonies* that her vow to Gracián makes her feel disloyal to previous confessors, making her sound a bit like an unfaithful wife suffering pangs of conscience. The confessor-penitent relationship could be extremely complex, as Jodi Bilinkoff points out, involving issues of sex, class, gender, and age.[19] It is not inconceivable that a momentary sexual tension existed between Teresa and Gracián. Yet, judging from the *Spiritual Testimonies,* it is more likely that Teresa considered Gracián a kind of divine gift to her, an answer to her prayer for a confessor who understood her and would provide coherent spiritual direction.

Gracián returned her affection, but the constant gossip to which he later became subject may have made him feel the need to clarify the chaste nature of their relationship:

...this great love I bore Madre Teresa of Jesus, and she for me, is a very different bond from what is usually had in the world, for that love is dangerous, vexatious and causes thoughts and temptations that slacken the spirit and disturb the senses. But this love that I had for Madre Teresa of Jesus and she for me produced in me purity, the spirit and love of God, and in her consolation and relief from her trials.[20]

Gracián seems concerned with the possibility that their friendship could be misinterpreted. He was clearly flattered by the attention of a leader of the reform whose reputation was growing rapidly, but his words reveal a level of discomfort. In *Peregrinación de Anastasio* he complains of the calumnies that her devotion to him caused him.[21] Likewise, Teresa felt the need to rationalize what must have seemed like a strange relationship: "It will seem inappropriate that he should have informed me of so many personal matters about his soul," she writes in *Foundations*. "At times he had reason for so doing because he thought that on account of my age and from what he had heard about me I had some experience."[22] They were right to be wary. In 1578, Gracián and María de San José were denounced to the Inquisition for immoral behavior.

If Teresa's intense devotion to the much younger Gracián has intrigued modern scholars, it is, at least in part, because it seems so out of character. From the time Teresa founded San José, the first Discalced Carmelite convent, in 1562, she demonstrated astonishing toughness and determination in the face of opposition. Church authorities did not embrace the reform with enthusiasm. Teresa's emphasis on the soul's intimate relationship with God pitted her against priests who feared the movement would undermine their influence. They found her meditative practices too similar to those of the Protestants and the *alumbrados,* a heretical sect that stressed divine illumination rather than religious ritual. Furthermore, Teresa claimed to experience visions, which provoked misgivings among clerics wary of ecstatics. The fact that she was a woman of *converso* origin heightened their distrust even more.[23] Before long, her emphasis on mental prayer and her supernatural experiences had attracted the attention of the Inquisition.

Among the Carmelite hierarchy, many resented her reformist efforts, viewing as arrogance her rejection of the status quo. Even her Carmelite sisters from the Convent of the Incarnation, where she had spent some twenty years, saw her breaking away and founding a new convent as a high-handed move. Yet, in spite of the obstacles, Teresa soldiered on, founding convent after convent, propelled by her clear vision and aided by her expert administrative abilities, level-headedness, people skills, and common sense. How could a woman with Teresa's smarts and political acumen be taken with a young man such as Gracián, whose imprudence had already aroused suspicion among both the Church and Carmelite hierarchy?

Almost from the beginning, Gracián displayed a dangerous impetuousness. Before he was thirty, he was named apostolic visitator with a commission to visit and reform the Carmelite convents of Andalusia—an area characterized by rowdiness among friars and hostility to the reforms being promoted by Rubeo. Buoyed by enthusiasm and prodded by his companion, Fray Ambrosio Mariano, he founded a convent at Almodóvar del Campo, thereby overstepping his authority; his job was to reform existing houses, not start new ones. The Provincial, Ángel de Salazar, ordered Gracián and Mariano back to Pastrana, but instead, they went to Seville, where Gracián claimed to have personal business. There, he infuriated discalced and calced alike by placing some discalced novices in a calced monastery.

When the disobedient friar ordered new monasteries created in Andalusia, he was flouting Rubeo's express orders that no further foundations be made in the south. Joachim Smet comments: "His concept of his office of apostolic commissary and visitor, later conferred on him, was that all things were permitted him in the name of reform."[24] Rubeo, clearly annoyed, scolded in a letter dated 26 April 1575, "You are scarcely a novice. Without knowledge of the institutions of the order, you may easily be led along ways and paths that are not good."[25] Nevertheless, against her better judgment, Teresa submitted to Gracián's authority and founded a convent in Seville, thereby exacerbating an already dicey situation. Frustrated by this unmanageable woman who seemed to have no respect for his position, Rubeo ordered Teresa to retire to one convent and to make no further foundations. A period of intense persecution of the discalced by the calced followed, during which Calced Carmelites arrested and imprisoned John of the Cross.

In hindsight, it seems inconceivable that Teresa would submit to the dominance of this reckless young friar, no matter how enthralled she was with his spiritual gifts. She admits in her *Book of Foundations* that she had severe reservations about going to Seville: "Since I saw that a foundation in Seville was the resolve of my major superior, I immediately submitted, although... I had some very serious reasons against [it]."[26] Why, then, did she go along with this badly conceived scheme? Researchers have tended to attribute her decision to her vow of obedience to Gracián, based on his own account. In his *Peregrinación,* Gracián describes how he tested Teresa's humility, submitting her to mortifications and sanctions to the point that she made no move without him. William Walsh wrote in his 1943 biography that she submitted to Gracián's orders with "all the generosity and confidence of a pure and childlike soul" and that "her obedience to Gracián, as the superior assigned to her by the Lord God, was so complete that test it as he would, he could never find a flaw in it."[27]

Likewise, Peers saw Teresa's decision to go to Seville simply as an act of obedience to Gracián.[28] Auclair suggests that the vow of obedience was an example of feminine wiliness: "Mother Teresa bent P. Jerónimo Gracián de la Madre de Dios to her will by the means all women employ, be they saints or sinners, geniuses or fools, to bring men under their dominations: she vowed obedience to him."[29] And once the vow was made, declares Auclair, Teresa had no choice but to go to Seville.[30]

In more recent years, scholars have offered a more multi-textured view of this relationship. Mary Luti, writing nearly five decades after Walsh, insists that although Teresa saw Gracián's faults, she "saw his perfection as crucial to the reform's progress… [Therefore], she could not give up on him any more than she could on the great ecclesiastical work God had given her to do."[31] For Luti, the "marriage" between Gracián and Teresa was a real marriage, albeit a rocky one; that is, an indissoluble union necessary to ensure the expansion of the reform. Efrén de la Madre de Dios and Otger Steggink argue that Teresa had to obey Gracián in his role of God's surrogate because it was God's will that the reform move forward, even in the face of opposition.[32] Cathleen Medwick notes that since Gracián was the apostolic visitator to the province and thereby her official superior, she really had no choice but to obey him. Medwick writes: "This, she perceived, was a grace the Lord had given her: to think that her superiors were always right."[33]

None of these scholars suggests that Teresa obeyed Gracián slavishly, but all of them see the vow of obedience as the instrument that placed her in an inferior position and that allowed him to prod her to Seville against her better judgment. Yet, it is possible that Teresa's submission to Gracián's authority has been overstated. To begin with, authority does not imply authoritarianism. In a spiritual context, submission to God is always unconditional, but submission to human beings is always conditional. In the Old Testament, disobedience to God, as described in Genesis, is the essence of sin. In the New Testament, Jesus' obedience to God is the source of salvation. Thus, obedience in a religious context is positive and liberating. Since obedience to human authority is understood as derived from God, all religious take a vow of obedience in imitation of Christ. However, such a vow does not imply blind submission to another's will, but submission to God though the authority He has delegated.[34]

Teresa's stipulation in her *Spiritual Testimonies* that her vow of obedience would apply only "to serious matters so as to avoid scruples" and only "so long as there was nothing in opposition to God or my superiors" displays a clear understanding of the limited nature of the vow of obedience.[35] She was not swearing blind allegiance to Gracián, but only promising to accept his direction in spiritual matters, and even then, only with respect to those issues she deemed important enough to discuss with him. She was clearly aware of the dangers of scrupulosity and of her responsibility to determine whether his commands were legitimate.

It is significant that Teresa had had Jesuit confessors and had made the *Spiritual Exercises,* and so would have been familiar with the kind of collaborative arrangement between priest and directee intrinsic to Jesuit spiritual practice.[36] The vehemence with which Teresa condemns the confessors who discounted her mystical experiences by attributing them to the devil, and the warmth with which she praises the Jesuits, suggest that she appreciated a priest-directee arrangement in which her views were taken seriously. In her article on the evolution of Teresa's *Vida,* Alison Weber suggests that even though Teresa wrote in obedience to spiritual directors, she worked with them collaboratively, for the most part retaining control of her words. With respect to the *Vida,* Weber notes that "the subsequent history of cordial correspondence between Teresa and the spiritual men suggest that we need to modulate the notion of censorship when speaking of spiritual autobiographies."[37] I would suggest that a similar reevaluation is needed with respect to vows of obedience, in particular Teresa's to Gracián. If, in spite of certain concerns for her freedom, Teresa agreed to make such a vow, it was because she believed the relationship would enrich her spiritually, not that it would obliterate her will.

Certainly, when Teresa obeyed Gracián's command to found in Seville, she did so both because he was the apostolic visitator and because she had taken a vow of obedience to him. However, she could have done otherwise. Since the order was made in defiance of Rubeo's directive, and she had stipulated that she would obey Gracián's commands only so long as there was nothing in them contrary to God *or her superiors,* she had grounds to refuse. She knew Rubeo had forbidden new foundations in Andalusia. The year before, she had written to María Bautista, Prioress of Valladolid, who thought Beas was in Andalusia: "You should know that Beas is not in Andalusia, but five miles this side, for I know that I cannot make foundations in Andalusia" (September 1574).[38] In *Foundations* she notes that if she had thought Beas was in Andalusia, she would never have founded there.[39] Teresa also knew that if she objected to the foundation, Gracián would not insist. She wrote to Bishop Mendoza: "I truly believe that he would not have placed me under any obligation, but his desire for this was so great that if I hadn't complied, I would have been left with a disturbing scruple that I wasn't being obedient, something I always desire to be" (11 May 1575).[40]

Although she casts her decision in the language of submission, several researchers (Alison Weber, Carole Slade, Gillian Ahlgren, Joan Cammarata) have shown how Teresa often achieved her objectives by maintaining a position of humility.[41] It seems possible that

Teresa was fully aware of what she was doing when she decided to found in Seville and honored Gracián's order because it coincided with her own desire to expand the reform. Although she was chary of Andalusia, three discalced friaries had already been founded in the south, and Teresa was happy with them.[42] Furthermore, she had already founded in Beas, which she now knew was, although under the civil jurisdiction of Castile, under the ecclesiastical jurisdiction of Andalusia. Perhaps, in spite of misgivings, she was now ready to take the next step.

But why frame her relationship with Gracián in terms of a spiritual marriage? Luti has written on Teresa's familiarity with the marriage customs of her time. However, this was not a conventional marriage. Marriage manuals, such as Juan Luis Vives' *Education of a Christian Woman,* stressed the duty of wives to obey their husbands. Although Vives claims that marriage should be viewed as a partnership, his guidelines suggest the opposite. He insists, for example, that a husband may beat a disobedient wife; if she is flogged undeservedly, the woman should accept her punishment gracefully and be grateful for the privilege of suffering like Christ. In his *The Institution of Marriage,* Erasmus takes a more moderate view, but still insists on male dominance. Still, the numerous women who worked side by side with their husbands as artisans—carpenters, shoemakers, bakers or farriers—suggests that for some couples even conventional marriage could be a collaboration. I think the language of marriage allowed Teresa both to legitimize her spiritual and emotional bond with Gracián and to endow it with a permanence which, after her difficult experiences with incompetent spiritual directors, she craved.

However, Teresa never played the "little wife." Pedra points out that although Saint Teresa felt affection for Gracián, she was astute enough to see that in terms of his apostolic responsibilities, he had his "ups and downs."[43] The fact is that in her relationship with Gracián, she assumed many roles—mother, collaborator, teacher, spiritual director, and defender—that placed her on equal footing with him, or even in a position of superiority, although she always treated him with tact and respect.

In many missives Teresa assumes the position of a hovering mother, showing keen concern for Gracián's health. She frequently warns him against overtaxing himself. In one letter she warns him not to work "like a Jesuit"—an order known for its rigor: "it's necessary that you realize that you are not made of iron, and that many in the Society have ruined themselves through overwork" (9 January 1577).[44] She advises him to rest sufficiently: "it seems to me that you are allowing yourself very little, for if you are going to Matins and getting up early, I don't know how you are getting enough sleep" (October 1577), and:

> I tell you, *mi padre,* that it would be good for you to get your sleep. Realize that you have a great deal of work, and the tiredness is not felt until the head gets into such a condition that there is no remedy, and you already know how important your health is… [W]hen it is time to sleep, set aside your projects, however necessary … (December 1577).[45]

Teresa clearly had no qualms about assuming dominance in her relationship with Gracián in matters concerning his physical well-being. Her own experience with health problems and the debilitating effects of overwork put her in a position to counsel (perhaps he would have said nag!) him on such issues. It is significant that, like several other nuns who enjoyed close relationships with priests, she often addresses him as "my son" in her letters, reversing the customary roles of "father" and spiritual "daughter."[46]

But it was not only on such neutral or "non-professional" issues as health that Teresa assumed a position of superiority. As her letters reveal, she clearly did not conform to the traditional "script" that proscribed women from instructing men in spiritual matters, but rather often assumed a degree of responsibility for Gracián's spiritual guidance. When she thinks Gracián is so overtired that he is neglecting his prayers, she writes: "[Paul] shouldn't get into the habit of abandoning so great a treasure... For the blessings the Lord gives in prayer are most remarkable, and I'm not surprised that the devil would like to take them away" (December 1577).[47] With respect to all the aggravation Gracián has to endure from the calced, she advises patience, for "God orders these things so his servants suffer" and it's not our place to question Him. "I understand what a martyr you've been, what with all their hostility," she adds, "but if you consider it, you'll see that God is guiding you" (15 October 1578).[48] Teresa was neither in awe of nor submissive to Gracián, but called upon her extensive experience guiding nuns to calm and encourage him in difficult situations.

She also guided him politically. Gracián had the title of visitator, with the authority that title conferred, but Teresa had the title of Foundress of the discalced, which also conferred authority. With respect to the female convents, her sex alone was enough to grant stature. Gracián routinely consulted her about visiting convents and, in fact, she composed *The Way to Visit Convents* to guide him in his visitations. The tone of her letters on this subject is confident and commanding: "You should be careful, *padre mío,* in this matter, and believe that I understand women's nature better than you" (October 1575).[49] Her advice includes instructions on dealing tactfully with Jesuits, using leniency toward nuns, and taking extreme care when assigning confessors. One subject on which she insists repeatedly is the ability of women to understand and guide other women. In this matter Gracián apparently accepted her authority, since he had her write *The Interior Castle* primarily for the enlightenment of other nuns.

Yet, as a woman working for reform within a larger organization, Teresa was often relatively powerless. She constantly had to navigate among higher-ups anxious to silence her, as when Rubeo ordered her to refrain from founding convents and to remain in Toledo, or when her provincial Ángel de Salazar excommunicated her as a result of her activities, or when Papal Nuncio Filippo Sega put the discalced under the authority of the calced. Through moves such as these, Teresa's superiors attempted to clip her wings. However, Teresa resisted their efforts in part by exercising—or endeavoring to exercise—control over Gracián, whom she used to further her ends. When Rubeo threatened to suppress the monasteries Gracián had founded in Andalusia under pain of excommunication, Teresa, a shrewd political strategist, wrote the Carmelite General a letter reminding him of Gracián's connections at Court, where both his father and brother served as secretaries to the king: "*Mi padre* and Lord, this is not a time for excommunications. Gracián has a brother close to the king who serves as his secretary and of whom the king is very fond. And the king from what I have learned might side with the reform" (18 June 1575).[50] When Rubeo backed down and allowed the visitations, Teresa wrote to Gracián urging him to go ahead and carry out his duties (27 September 1575).[51]

The calced Andalusian friars were vehement in their opposition to Rubeo's reforms, which Gracián, as visitor, was to implement.[52] Gracián would have preferred not to deal with the mitigated friars at all and, in fact, tried to convince Ormaneto to divide the order.[53] With a keen understanding of human psychology, Teresa tried to guide Gracián, writing to him on 27 September 1575 that the Andalusian

Carmelites would accept his authority over them, provided he treaded carefully: "...all of them are determined to obey your paternity and help you in suppressing any sinful abuses, as long as there are no extreme solutions taken in regard to other matters."[54] Gracián had promised to consult with Teresa in matters concerning the order, but just as her obedience to him left room for maneuvering, so did his pledge to her. On 21 November 1575, when Gracián began his visitation of the Casa Grande in Seville, the Calced Carmelites raised a ruckus, bolting the door and refusing to let him leave. Gracián, according to his own description of these events in *Peregrinaciones*, thought they were going to kill him. Instead of heeding Teresa's advice to avoid "extreme solutions," Gracián began to consider measures to bully them into submission, including excommunication. Teresa, certain that a tough stance would provoke undesirable results, warned against it: "You should hold off, even if they do not obey, from delivering letters of excommunication, so that they may have time to reflect" (November 1575).[55] Fifteen years of grappling with powerful men had taught her the danger of direct confrontation.

However, Gracián decided to force the issue and did in fact excommunicate the friars. On 30 December 1575 Teresa complained to María Bautista, "There is no obedience; he has excommunicated them; there is another uproar. I tell you I have had much more suffering than happiness since he has been here; things were going much better before."[56] Teresa had given Gracián her opinion, and she expected him to acquiesce. She clearly interpreted Gracián's promise to consult her on matters concerning the order as an obligation, but not only did Gracián disregard her advice, he joined Rubeo in insisting she go to Toledo and stay there. She complains to María Bautista: "Father visitator has not allowed me to leave here because for now he has more authority over me than our most Reverend Father General. I don't know where it will all end up" (30 December 1575).[57] Teresa's resentment of Gracián is manifest in the letters of this period. His highhandedness had exacerbated conflicts within the order and had placed constraints on her movement. If Teresa was momentarily enthralled with Gracián when she met him in Beas, by the end of 1575 she was thoroughly aggravated with him.

In fall of the following year, Gracián was expending what Teresa considered an inordinate amount of energy on some of the smaller Andalusian monasteries, which were not reforming fast enough to suit him. On 20 September she wrote a letter scolding him for his impatience and for putting himself in a vulnerable position: "Do not think, *mi padre,* that you can make things perfect with one stroke… Hardly will you have left when they will return to their former ways, and by doing this are exposing yourself to a thousand dangers."[58] But if Gracián was compulsive about the visitations, he was dragging his heels on another matter: the division of the Carmelites. In order to extricate themselves from calced control, the discalced would have to break off into a separate province, an operation that would involve intricate negotiations. Rubeo had firmly opposed such a move, insisting that "no rift should be created in the order by calling some discalced and others 'of the cloth.'"[59] Even so, Teresa urged Gracián to send two Discalced friars to Rome to petition the Nuncio for the partition. Acutely aware that time was of the essence because the Nuncio was mortally ill, Teresa wrote to Gracián "Your paternity should make every effort that they not delay in going… Don't take this as a secondary matter" (20 September 1576).[60] Although she was officially cloistered in Toledo, Teresa was able to maneuver politically by manipulating Gracián—to a degree.

But Gracián was not so easy to control. His lack of common sense must have infuriated Teresa, who reprimanded him time and again. In October 1576 she reproaches him for failing to make known a brief from the Nuncio appointing him apostolic visitator of the Calced Carmelites in Andalusia, a document that would have established his authority over them: "In regard to what you said in your letter about... why you did not send the brief, certainly if there were reason for doubt, it would have been better to think of this beforehand" (21 October 1576).[61] In one of Gracián's clumsiest gaffs, he thoughtlessly shared one of Teresa's confidential letters with some companions. Although Teresa must have been beside herself, she chides him tactfully, "And since you understand the love with which I say this, you can pardon me and do me the favor I've asked of you: not to read in public the letters I write to you. Remember that people interpret things differently and that superiors should never be so open about some matters" (November 1576).[62]

As her correspondence makes clear, Teresa was not so enthralled with Gracián that she failed to see his many weaknesses or that she accepted his direction uncritically. And yet, during this entire period she was usually quick to defend him. In August 1575, even though she had already had a taste of Gracián's impetuousness, she wrote to her sister: "You ought also to know that they have given Padre Gracián authority over all the discalced friars and nuns down here and up there as well; no better thing could have happened for us. He is the ideal person..." (12 August 1575).[63] A few days later, she wrote to María Bautista, who had apparently criticized Gracián's recklessness in Andalusia: "If you find faults in him, it will be because you have not spoken much with him and don't know him well. I tell you he is a saint and not at all impetuous, but very cautious. I already have experience of that..." (28 August 1575).[64]

Like a fond mother, Teresa criticizes Gracián but constantly makes excuses for him to others. She reminds the nuns repeatedly how lucky they are to have him with them and begs María de San José to take special precautions for his health and well-being. When Gracián's enemies issue a libelous document accusing him of indiscretions with María de San José and other nuns, Teresa audaciously writes to King Philip II on his behalf:

> News has reached me that a memorandum was delivered to your majesty against Padre Maestro Gracián. I am astonished at the intrigues of the devil and these calced fathers. They're not satisfied with defaming this servant of God (for he truly is and has so edified us that the monasteries he has visited always write to me about how he has left them with a new spirit), but they are striving now to discredit these monasteries where God is well served (18 September 1577).[65]

Teresa knew very well that Gracián's visitations did not always leave his friars edified, but the allegations threatened to seriously undermine the reform. Besides, in spite of the aggravation he caused her, she was sincerely fond of him.

Her affection is apparent in many of her letters, including those in which she scolds him. Although she was careful to observe the rules of etiquette in her correspondence, addressing him respectfully as Your Reverence, Your Paternity, or less formally, My Father, she was comfortable enough in their relationship to tease him. An expert rider (women in those days rode mules), Teresa chides Gracián about his propensity to fall from his mount: "…it would be good if they tied you to the saddle so that you couldn't fall. I don't know what kind of donkey that is…" (October 1575).[66] Having met his mother, she writes to him: "She has a simplicity and openness that put me in seventh heaven. In these she greatly surpasses her son" (20 September 1576).[67]

Many of her letters are full of playfulness and banter. Others attest to her willingness to break the rules for him, as when she writes to María de San José to serve him dinner in the convent parlor, a privilege not normally accorded priests, or when she supports his efforts to have his underage sister, Isabel, admitted to the order. During the rest of her life Teresa continued to write to Gracián, giving him news about her foundations, inquiring about his health and reporting on her own, or scolding him for some inappropriate decision. Often she complains about his failure to write her, revealing just how much his silence hurt her.

Like most human relationships, the bond between Teresa and Gracián was variegated and fluctuating. Teresa neither trusted Gracián like an innocent child nor was able to judge him with complete objectivity. If she was fleetingly infatuated with him, she soon became conscious of his shortcomings. Yet, her affection for him remained strong in spite of her awareness of his flaws. Although she accepted him as her superior, what role he played in her spiritual development is unclear. She already had a developed notion of her own spirituality before she met him. However, he was her collaborator in the reform during the last decade and a half of her life. In this relationship, Teresa's role was more that of mother—bossy and scolding, yet loving and indulgent—than of obedient wife.

---

[1]   The Andalusian Carmelites were notoriously lax, and the Carmelite General, Giovanni Battista Rossi (known in Spanish as Rubeo), was trying to impose reforms on them. The papal nuncio, Niccoló Ormaneto, had written to the Pope's secretary that it would be necessary to exert pressure on the Andalusian Carmelites to keep them under control. For that reason, visitations were necessary. However, the apostolic visitor, the Dominican Francisco Vargas, did not "have the stomach" for the job, so Ormaneto appointed Vargas and Gracián to serve *in solidum*. See Joachim Smet, O.Carm., *The Carmelites: A History of the Brothers of Our Lady of Mount Carmel*, vol. 2. (Darien, Il: Carmelite Spiritual Center, 1982), 64. For a brief biography of Gracián, see *Just Man, Husband of Mary, Guardian of Christ:*

An Anthology of Readings from Jerónimo Gracián's <u>Summary of the Excellencies of St. Joseph</u> (1597), ed. and trans. Joseph F. Chorpenning, O.S.F.S. (Philadelphia: Saint Joseph's University Press, 1993), 5-17.

2   *The Collected Letters of St. Teresa of Ávila*, trans. Kieran Kavanaugh, O.C.D., vol. 1. Washington, D.C.: ICS, 2001 (volume 2 is forthcoming), 1:202. Unless otherwise indicated, translations of Teresa's letters are taken from this edition, hereafter abbreviated as Kavanaugh.

3   Kavanaugh, 1:207 and 1:199.

4   Kavanaugh, 1:423. In Teresa's time couriers were sometimes ambushed and their cargo stolen. Because she feared her letters would be intercepted by "friars of the cloth" (Calced Carmelites) or other enemy forces, Teresa used code names in her correspondence to protect her collaborators in the reform.

5   Kavanaugh, 1:439.

6   Mary Luti, "'A Marriage Well-Arranged': Teresa of Ávila and Fray Jerónimo Gracián de la Madre de Dios," *Studia Mystica* 10 (1989): 32-46, at 35.

7   Marcelle Auclair, *Saint Teresa of Ávila*, trans. Kathleen Pond (Petersham, MA: St. Bede's Publications, 1988), 258.

8   E. Allison Peers, *Mother of Carmel: A Portrait of St. Teresa de Jesús* (Gorham, NY: Morehouse, 1946), 122.

9   Smet, 65.

10   José Alberto Pedra, *Jerónimo Gracián de la Madre de Dios: o herdeiro exilado* (Curitiba: Artes e Textos, 2003), 46-47, translation mine.

11   Teresa of Ávila, *Book of Her Foundations,* 24.1. Unless otherwise indicated, all translations of Teresa's books are taken from *The Collected Works of St. Teresa of Ávila*, trans. Kieran Kavanaugh and Otilio Rodríguez, 3 vols. (Washington, D.C.: ICS Publications, 1976-85) and are referenced by chapter and section number.

12   Alfonso Ruiz, "La correspondencia de Gracián con Santa Teresa vista desde el epistolario teresiano," in *El Padre Gracián: Discípulo, amigo, provincial de Santa Teresa* (Burgos: Monte Carmelo, 1984), 59-108, translation mine. In fact, there are many examples of close friendships between nuns and their confessors or spiritual directors, among them those of Saint Francis of Assisi (1181?-1226) and Saint Clare (1194-1253), the Blessed Angela of Foligno (d. 1309) and Fra Arnaldo, and Ana María de San José (d. 1632) and Martín García (d. 1640). See Jane Tar, "Angela of Foligno as a Potential Model for Franciscan Women Religious in Early Modern Spain," forthcom-

ing in *Magistra,* and the same author's "Spiritual Counsel and the Bonds of Affection: A Study and Translation of Four Letters by a Spanish, Mystical Nun," forthcoming in *Mystics Quarterly.*

[13] Teresa of Ávila, *Spiritual Testimonies,* 35.1-2. Teresa often refers to herself as an anonymous third person.

[14] Teresa of Ávila, *Spiritual Testimonies,* 36.2.

[15] Teresa of Ávila, *Spiritual Testimonies,* 36.7.

[16] Kavanaugh, 1:464.

[17] Luti, 36.

[18] Auclair, 260.

[19] Jodi Bilinkoff, "Confession, Gender, Life-Writing: Some Cases (Mainly) from Spain," in *Penitence in the Age of Reformations,* ed. Katharine Jackson Lualdi and Anne T. Thayer (Aldershot: Ashgate, 2000), 169-83, at 180-81.

[20] Jerónimo Gracián de la Madre de Dios, O.C.D., *Peregrinación de Anastasio,* ed. Giovanni Maria Bertini (Barcelona: Juan Flors, 1966). A more recent edition of Gracián's text was published in 2001 (Rome: Teresianum); Diálogo 16. In September, 1577, Baltasar de Nieto circulated a libelous document against Gracián accusing him of immoral conduct with some of the discalced nuns. Rumors circulated about Gracián's supposed relations with María de San José, some of the wealthy women to whom he was confessor, and even Teresa herself. Teresa wrote a letter, dated 18 September 1577, to King Phillip II defending Gracián and condemning his accusers.

[21] Gracián, Diálogo 1 in *Peregrinación.*

[22] Teresa of Ávila, *Foundations,* 23.11. As Tar has shown in the articles cited above, women often assumed positions of authority in heterosexual spiritual friendships.

[23] *Conversos* were Christians of Jewish origin.

[24] Smet, 61.

[25] Quoted in Smet, 62.

[26] *Foundations,* 24.4.

[27] William Thomas Walsh, *Saint Teresa of Ávila* (Rockford, IL: Tan, 1943), 444 and 445.

[28] Peers, 123.

[29] Auclair, 262.

[30] Auclair, 268.

[31] Luti, 39.

[32] Efren de la Madre de Dios, O.C.D. and Otger Steggink, O.Carm., *Tiempo y vida de Santa Teresa* (Madrid: Biblioteca de Autores Cristianos, 1996), 607.

[33] Cathleen Medwick, *Teresa of Ávila: The Progress of a Soul* (New York: Knopf, 1999), 185.

[34] In the sixteenth century, many people made vows of obedience, not just religious. Since the will of God was identified with the institutional form of authority, submission to a priest was seen as a means of spiritual purification that freed the individual from the interference of the ego. However, the conditional nature of this submission meant that those who made vows of obedience still had use of their judgment and consciences.

[35] Teresa of Ávila, *Spiritual Testimonies*, 36.7.

[36] Ignatius of Loyola lays out guidelines for priests directing the Spiritual Exercises that promote cooperation between director and directee. Annotation 15 of the instructions for spiritual directors states that the director "ought not to move the one receiving [the Exercises] more to poverty or to any particular promise than to their contraries," that is, not to try to influence the directee unduly. The very first line of the instructions for the First Week of the Exercises refers to the priest-directee relationship as a collaboration and suggests both approach the experience with good will and an open mind: "So that the director and the exercitant may collaborate better…, it must be presupposed that any good Christian has to be more ready to justify than to condemn a neighbor's statement." In his letters on obedience, Ignatius stresses that one is never obligated to follow a command he believes to be contrary to God, and in his Reminiscences and letters he warns against excessive scrupulosity. Ignatius of Loyola, *Personal Writings,* trans. and ed. Joseph A. Munitiz and Philip Endean (London: Penguin, 1996), 286 and 289.

[37] Alison Weber, "The Three Lives of the *Vida:* The Uses of Convent Autobiography," in *Women, Texts and Authority in the Early Modern Spanish World,* ed. Marta V. Vicente and Luis R. Corteguera (Aldershot: Ashgate, 2003), 110.

[38] Kavanaugh, 1:182.

[39] Teresa of Ávila, *Foundations,* 24.4.

[40] Kavanaugh, 1:200.

[41] See Alison Weber, *Teresa of Ávila and the Rhetoric of Femininity* (Princeton: Princeton University Press, 1990); Carole Slade, *St. Teresa of Ávila: Author of a Heroic Life* (Berkeley: University of California Press, 1995); Gillian T.W. Ahlgren, *Teresa of Ávila and the Politics of Sanctity* (Ithaca and London: Cornell University Press, 1996); and Joan Cammerata,

"El discurso femenino de Santa Teresa de Ávila, defensora de la mujer renacentista," *Actas Irvine* 92, Asociación Internacional de Hispanistas (Irvine, CA: University of California, 1994), 58-65, and the same author's "Mystical Psychagogue, Cultural Other: St. Teresa of Ávila," in *Homenaje a Bruno Damiani,* ed. Filippo María Toscano (Lanham, MD: University Press of America, 1994), 31-42.

[42] Smet, 65.

[43] Pedra, 45.

[44] Kavanaugh, 1:463.

[45] Kavanaugh, 1:572 and 1:577.

[46] As Tar demonstrates in the articles cited above, such role reversal was not uncommon.

[47] Kavanaugh, 1:577-78.

[48] Teresa of Ávila, *Epistolario,* ed. Luis Rodríguez Martínez and Teófanes Egido (Madrid: Espiritualidad), 575, translation mine.

[49] Kavanaugh, 1:233.

[50] Kavanaugh, 1:208.

[51] Kavanaugh, 1:227-29.

[52] The Andalusian friars were known to circulate in regular street clothes, to engage in gambling and brawling, and to keep the company of prostitutes. The Pope demanded that Rubeo impose discipline on them. See note 1.

[53] Smet, 71.

[54] Kavanaugh, 1:227.

[55] Kavanaugh, 1:241.

[56] Kavanaugh, 1:245.

[57] Kavanaugh, 1:245-46.

[58] Kavanaugh, 1:327-28.

[59] Quoted in Smet, 68.

[60] Kavanaugh, 1:330. In 1581, one year before Teresa's death, King Phillip II had a brief issued separating the calced and discalced into separate provinces. From this time on, the Calced and Discalced (or Mitigated) were separate orders and their names written with capitals.

[61] Kavanaugh, 1:356.

[62] Kavanaugh, 1:379.

[63] Kavanaugh, 1:220.

[64] Kavanaugh, 1:224.

[65] Kavanaugh, 1:562.

[66] Kavanaugh, 1:235.

[67] Kavanaugh, 1:328.

Heeding the 'Madre': Ana de San Agustín and the Voice of Santa Teresa

Elizabeth Teresa Howe
Tufts University
Institutum Carmelitanum

In the prologue to the first edition of Santa Teresa's complete works (1588), Fray Luis de León observed to Ana de Jesús, the prioress of the Discalced Carmelite nuns in Madrid: "I did not know nor see Mother Teresa of Jesus while she was on earth but now that she lives in heaven I know and see her in two living images that she left us of herself, which are her daughters and her books; which, in my judgement, are also faithful witnesses, without exception, to her great virtue."[1]

The works and authors gathered in this collection demonstrate the perspicacity of Fray Luis's observation, for clearly the men and women who embraced the Teresian reform continued the influence of Santa Teresa long after her death in 1582. Certainly those like Ana de Jesús, who had known the foundress in life, imitated Santa Teresa not only in the life they chose but often in the very works—literary and otherwise—that they undertook. These included the foundation of new houses of the reform throughout Europe and beyond, as well as the composition of texts as diverse as those that flowed from the hand of the saint.

Among the best known of Santa Teresa's early followers who continued the work of the Discalced reform are María de San José, Ana de San Bartolomé and Ana de Jesús as well as Jerónimo Gracián. Yet, as a quick perusal of Manuel Serrano y Sanz's *Apuntes para una biblioteca de Escritoras Españolas (Notes for a Library of Spanish*

45

Women Writers) demonstrates, there are numerous works attributed to other Carmelite women writers of the period which also testify to the presence of Santa Teresa in a variety of forms.[2] They range from depositions pursuant to the beatification and canonization processes of the saint to *relaciones, vidas,* poems, letters, and the like. Although in some cases they are not of great literary value, they are nonetheless invaluable for the insight they provide about both the reform and women's writing in early modern Spain.

One among these authors is Madre Ana de San Agustín (1555-1624) who, like Ana de Jesús and the other notables mentioned earlier, knew Santa Teresa in life and testified to her continued influence in a number of ways. Ana de Pedruja was born in Pisuegra in the province of Valladolid in December 1555. Her father, Juan de Pedruja y Rebolledo, served as *administrador* to the Conde de Buendía at the time of her birth. In 1562 the entire family moved to the count's ancestral home of Dueñas not far from Valladolid. There they occupied a house close to an Augustinian church and monastery.

In the first of her two *relaciones,* Ana describes her life principally in terms of the visions she received. In fact, the first event she mentions is a vision of the Child Jesus that she received at the age of eleven. Subsequently, she decided to enter religious life but was unsure of which order to choose. What convinced her was the passage of a procession of Carmelites accompanied by the same figure of the Child Jesus she had seen in her earlier vision. When in 1568 a group of Carmelite nuns under the direction of Santa Teresa traveled from the monastery at Medina del Campo to establish a new foundation in Valladolid, Ana became better acquainted with the reform and the life it represented. With the blessing of her parents and the encouragement of Santa Teresa, she joined the new foundation at Malagón in 1575. There she professed her vows in May 1578 in the presence of Santa

Teresa, taking the name Ana de San Agustín.

Given Ana's predilection for an intense interior life, one marked by an extraordinary number of visions narrated in her two *relaciones,* the choice of the Teresian reform is not surprising. As Alison Weber remarks in her introduction to María de San José's *Book for the Hour of Recreation,* the Discalced Carmelites "believed that their reform was part of God's providential plan, that he communicated with them through supernatural visions and locutions, and that when necessary, he consoled them with ecstatic assurance of his presence."[3] Yet, as Weber also points out in her work on Teresa's rhetoric, the saint was chary, if not downright terrified, of visions and the possibility of diabolical illusions visited on gullible women. Weber explains that "diabolical seduction, seen as sexual possession by the devil, was emerging as the Inquisition's preferred explanation for ecstatic trances and other extraordinary phenomena."[4] Besides a desire to avoid undue scrutiny from the Inquisitors, Santa Teresa also feared that opponents of the reform might use claims to visionary experience against her and her followers.[5]

It is in the context of Santa Teresa's conflicted attitude toward visions and locutions that Ana de San Agustín's life in Carmel should be viewed. In 1579 the saint returned to Malagón in order to quiet some of the turmoil besetting the house. Ana was a part of at least some of this tumult since around the time of her profession she describes demonic interventions ostensibly designed to thwart her taking of vows.[6] For example, she describes how "one time demons threw me down the stairs," an event that mirrors a similar occurrence recorded about Santa Teresa by her cousin.[7]

As part of her visit to the Malagón house, the saint recruited some of the nuns to accompany her to a new foundation at Villanueva de la Jara. Ana de San Agustín was one of them. Before leaving

Villanueva, Santa Teresa appointed Ana to the posts of sacristan, cellarer, and portress, offices she held for nine years before being elected prioress in 1596.[8] As part of the dedication of the new foundation, the saint also installed a statue of the Child Jesus, a custom and devotion favored by her and her followers. Ana took charge of the statue and kept it near the turn during her term as portress. She records numerous occasions in which the figure spoke to her or intervened to assist her in her duties.

Heretofore, the direct influence of Santa Teresa on the life of Ana de San Agustín is evident. Not only in her choice of the Carmelite reform but also in her devotion to the *"Niño Jesús"* and her visionary experiences, Ana's life mirrors that of the founding Mother. When later as foundress and first prioress of a new house in Valera de Abajo, she was directed by her confessor and the Father Provincial of the Discalced to provide an account of her life, her imitation of the saint took on concrete form. The two *relaciones* transcribed by a fellow nun offer further evidence of the continued influence of Santa Teresa even after her death in 1582.

More importantly, the demand for an accounting of Ana's interior life by her confessor reflects the power relationships of male-female, confessor-nun, already apparent in Santa Teresa's composition of her own *Vida*. Ruth El Saffar asserts that during this period in Spain's history "autobiography originates out of the desire of those in power to acquaint themselves with those portions of the population who represent contact with that which the dominant powers have subordinated or oppressed. By demanding the autobiography, the confessor seeks to know the hidden world of the visionary. The inquisitor seeks to ferret out the secrets of the witch or renegade."[9] As was the case with the saint, so, too, with Ana de San Agustín, the autobiographical confession comes in response to authority. Yet, in the telling,

Ana invokes higher authorities to validate the truthfulness of what is related. In this respect, Santa Teresa proves to be an important player in her *relación*.

Ana de San Agustín's reputation as a clairvoyant predated Santa Teresa's death, a fact to which she attested in the *procesos* surrounding the beatification. There Ana testified to visions she had of Santa Teresa which occurred at different stages of her acquaintance with the saint. They included seeing Teresa's communication with the Child Jesus, her experience of heavenly music, and her apparition to Ana by night in Malagón even though the saint was still in Ávila.[10] Clearly Ana was predisposed to "see" Santa Teresa as a guide and exemplar even before the latter's death. After October 1582, Ana de San Agustín continued to receive visions and locutions from the saint as, indeed, did other members of the reform. But Ana's experience of Santa Teresa in the course of these visions is distinct from that recorded by other Carmelites, since the Teresa who appears to her seems a more forbidding figure than the one encountered by the likes of Ana de San Bartolomé or Ana de Jesús. Nevertheless, like her sisters in Carmel, Ana responded to these visitations in the same way that she had when Santa Teresa was alive. For Ana, the posthumous authority of the foundress, which superseded that of living priests and confessors, demanded the same level of obedience that she had proffered her in life.

Probably the best known of Ana's visions are those of hell and heaven. A series of preliminary visions, however, precedes them. In these earlier appearances, the saint instructs Ana, rather forcefully, to admonish some among the Discalced who make claims that border on the heretical.[11] When Ana takes no action on the directive, the saint reappears twice more, each time urging with greater vehemence that she communicate the message to her superiors. As Ana continues to desist, the sufferings visited on her mimic those of the damned. She finds herself surrounded by "a large number of demons who furiously began to torture her with many terrible torments."[12] This combination of visions—of the saint and of the devil—is initially perplexing. In the context of Santa Teresa's admonition and the probable source of confusion about her teachings, however, all is clarified, for the saint appears to take seriously quietist and neo-Cathar tendencies among some of her followers. For Ana de San Agustín, caution is called for in order to assure herself that she is not deluded by the present vision of her foundress.

Finally, the event that precipitates her main vision of hell revolves around the death of Nicolás Doria and the selection of Elías de San Martín as General in 1594. At this critical juncture, Ana is transported by the saint and a recently deceased Discalced friar to a wide and spacious road. There Santa Teresa commands her once more to instruct her superiors to choose leaders who will zealously observe the Rule.[13] Next, the saint and friar place her on a much narrower road and then abandon her to "many demons" (*"muchos demonios"*), who, in turn, carry her to hell.

The details Ana provides of this series of visions are evocative of some passages to be found in the *Vida* of Santa Teresa. These include the apparent inversion of the image of the "strait and narrow road" from that which leads to heaven to that which, instead, reaches hell. The comparison of hell to a pool of filthy, pest-ridden water also recalls the saint's description.[14] Both Ana and Santa Teresa receive their respective visions of hell at moments of crisis in the Discalced reform: Santa Teresa in connection with the foundation of the first house of the reform at San José de Ávila and Ana in the transition from Doria's generalship to that of Elías de San Martín.

Even the descriptions of hell by each woman share similar details. Santa Teresa describes the scene in her *Vida (The Book of Her Life)*:

> The entrance, I thought, resembled a very long, narrow passage, like a furnace, very low, dark and closely confined; the ground seemed to be full of water which looked like filthy, evil-smelling mud, and in it were many wicked-looking reptiles. At the end there was a hollow place scooped out of a wall, like a cupboard, and it was here that I found myself in close confinement.[15]

The saint goes on to describe her own "bodily sufferings"[16] and the terror this vision induced. In Ana's case, she writes:

> at the end of this long, narrow passage I saw at the further end another, deeper center that was the pit of hell full of fire and demons and surrounded by terrible confusion to the sight and very frightening to my soul . . . I saw that poisonous toads entered and exited through the senses of those tortured souls.[17]

The common elements include the narrow entrance, the blazing furnace or oven, filthy water, reptiles, and the overarching terror of the place.

Unlike Santa Teresa, Ana continues her account with detailed descriptions of the damned and their torments. She focuses primarily on ecclesiastical and monastic sinners. When she describes the sufferings of monks and nuns, she seems to relish the details of their torments. Included is an especially harsh punishment visited upon a friar and a nun of the order who, having sinned together, now suffer together in the pit of hell. Hence, her infernal vision provides specific examples of punishment for those who stray from orthodoxy as Santa Teresa had directed her to communicate to her monastic companions. By implication, these details confirm the validity of Ana's claims to visitations and communications from the saint as well.

The vision of heaven follows immediately that of hell. Not surprisingly, its description is the antithesis of hell's. At the same time, the souls to be found in heaven parallel the population of hell with the obvious difference that they are rewarded for their virtuous lives. Among the saved are Santa Teresa, placed there before the Church had officially ruled on her case, and Ana's own parents. Once again, Ana reflects similar passages in the saint's *Vida*. Santa Teresa writes: "I thought I was being carried up to Heaven: the first persons I saw there were my father and mother, and such great things happened in so short a time . . . that I was completely lost to myself, and thought it too great a favor."[18] More importantly, the saint also expresses her fear that it might be an illusion, so that she is embarrassed and afraid to tell her confessor. She finally relents and tells him, and, he, in turn, reassures her.

Whether from similar motives or not, Ana, too, indicates her reluctance to tell her confessor the totality of this vision. Rather, she limits herself to what she saw of hell and what she was ordered to communicate by Santa Teresa. She is punctilious in her obedience. Although she indicates that she was also transported to heaven, she withholds from the confessor the details of that part of the vision. She only reveals them when she narrates her *relación*. The selective nature of her account attests to some measure of authorial control, however slight, over her life story.

Significantly, as Ana concludes her narrative, she returns to the events that precipitated it, reminding her readers that the saint had admonished both friars and nuns to adhere to "the rule, constitutions, and obligations" (*"la regla, constituçiones y obligaçiones"*) of the order. She implies that those members of the reform who observe these carefully and who imitate the foundress' virtues, especially obedience, will share in the beatific vision. Those who do not will occupy the roiled waters of the pool into which Santa Teresa threatened to push Ana for her disobedience. It is a curious message, given her own reluctance to be entirely forthcoming. Nevertheless, the authority for her assertions is no less a figure than the saint herself.

Subsequent visions of Santa Teresa in the course of the *relaciones* almost always occur in connection with the business of the reform or with strict adherence to the rule.[19] For Ana de San Agustín, Santa Teresa's directives are a means of authorizing her message to her superiors. Thus, she witnesses *"nuestra madre"* ("our mother" Santa Teresa) happily collecting the ballots that lead to the election of Alonso de Jesús María as general of the order (coincidentally, it is Alonso who receives the two *relaciones*.).[20] In another vision, the saint appears in the refectory and admonishes Ana for eating chicken, thereby "relaxing" the rule.[21] In a third, she thanks Ana for the assistance given in the canonization process.[22]

In contrast to the very active role taken by Ana de Jesús, María de San José, and Ana de San Bartolomé in the governance issues facing the nuns after Santa Teresa's death, Ana de San Agustín's involvement is at once removed and opaque. She never reveals directly which side she supports in this ongoing discussion, yet she invokes Santa Teresa at virtually every instance as the authority behind whatever view she does advance. In one further, revealing account, however, Ana suggests her allegiance to the interpretation of the saint's intent advanced by Doria and Ana de San Bartolomé.[23] Since she was close to Ana de San Bartolomé, it is not surprising. Nevertheless, the manifestation of her allegiance is oblique at best.

Almost as an afterthought, she relates a vision she had in Villanueva de la Jara during a visitation by the Father Provincial. As the friar examines the account books Ana witnesses the Mother of God (*"Madre de Dios"*) gazing at him with a scowl on her face and removing the habit from him in disgust.[24] Having noticed a reaction in Ana's own face, the friar presses her to explain it. When she does, he promises to reform his ways, but Ana comments that "after this event some six of seven years later, more or less, he was thrown out of the order."[25] Although she does not identify the friar, it was presumably Jerónimo Gracián, who was expelled by Doria for his apparent laxity or for his disobedience to his superiors.[26] Interestingly, it is the Virgin Mary who dismisses the friar and not Santa Teresa. Given the real affection the saint had for Gracián, it is not surprising that she does not appear in this vision. By the same token, it is not clear in the *relación* whether Ana benefits from clairvoyance or hindsight, since the expulsion occurred some six or seven years after the visitation of the convent but is only revealed in this account, almost fourteen years after the fact.

Narration of the visions, locutions, and other events in the life of Ana de San Agustín came about, as was usually the case with women religious of the time, in response to requests from her religious superiors. As was true for Santa Teresa, the superior in question was invariably a male confessor or Provincial. Ana apparently resisted as long as she could from complying with the demand to account for her interior life. She remarks near the end of the first *relación* on her "rebellion often against obeying those prelates who demand of her the mortification of writing about these things."[27] Her confessor, Fray Juan de San José, requires an account from her, one which she tries to avoid. When she finally attempts to commit it to writing, she claims that "[while] actually writing, the pages were burned up without my seeing who [did it]."[28] This act of spontaneous combustion occurs two more times so that she claims to be unable to complete the task for her confessor. Rather than an example of diabolical intervention or of spontaneous combustion, however, this event suggests an overt act of rebellion on Ana's part to avoid commiting her visions to writing. At the same time, it is a wonderfully ironic inversion of the actual destruction by fire of some of Santa Teresa's writings by her confessor, Padre Yanguas.[29] When Alonso de Santa María renews the demand, she experiences yet another destruction by fire of her manuscript, then fails to attempt another redaction since, as she explains, she found herself "excused since it was the last year of his provincialate."[30] Finally, she produces a version that does not burst into flame, a result which she believes attests to the veracity of what she has written.[31]

As this brief introduction to Ana de San Agustín's life and works attempts to demonstrate, the voice of Santa Teresa and, more importantly, her influence pervades the experience of her earliest followers. In her two *relaciones,* Ana credits the saint with playing a pivotal role, not only in her life but in that of the order as well. She invokes the foundress as the ultimate authority for virtually all that she undertakes, thus making her visible to the likes of Fray Luis de León and those others who did not know the *Madre* in life. She also heeds her counsel and establishes a claim to serve as mediator between her religious superiors and the foundress as the reform continues to grow and expand. Thus, through her visions and locutions, Ana was able to lay claim to an authoritative position in her own right as prioress, foundress, builder, and, finally, autobiographer.

---

[1]   Luis de León, *Obras completas castellanas,* vol. 1: *El Cantar de los Cantares, La perfecta casada, Los nombres de Cristo, Escritos varios,* ed. Félix García,

O.S.A. (Madrid: Editorial Católica, 1977), 904; my translation.

2   Manuel Serrano y Sanz, *Apuntes para una biblioteca de Escritoras Españolas,* 4 vols. (Madrid: Rivadeneyra, 1903).

3   María de San José Salazar, *Book for the Hour of Recreation,* introduction and notes by Alison Weber, trans. Amanda Powell (Chicago and London: University of Chicago Press, 2002), 15.

4   Alison Weber, *Teresa of Ávila and the Rhetoric of Femininity* (Princeton: Princeton University Press, 1990), 45.

5   Consider Weber's comment that "Teresa attributes interpersonal conflict— especially the internecine struggle with the Calced—to diabolical interven- tion," in Alison Weber, "Santa Teresa, Demonologist," in *Culture and Control in Counter-Reformation Spain,* ed. Anne J. Cruz and Mary Elizabeth Perry (Minneapolis: University of Minnesota Press, 1992), 171-95, at 180.

6   Ana de San Agustín, *The Visionary Life of Madre Ana de San Agustín,* ed. Elizabeth Teresa Howe (Suffolk, England: Tamesis Press, 2004), 52-53.

7   Ana de San Agustín, 53; "una ves me echaron [los demonios] unas escaleras abajo." See *Complete Works of Saint Teresa of Jesus,* ed. and trans. E. Allison Peers, 3 vols. (London: Sheed and Ward, 1946), 3:344, n. 1.

8   The events surrounding the foundation at Villanueva de la Jara can be found in ch. 28 of Teresa's *Book of Her Foundations.*

9   Ruth El Saffar, *Rapture Encaged: The Suppression of the Feminine in Western Culture* (London and New York: Routledge, 1994), 72.

10 See Efrén de la Madre de Dios, O.C.D. and Otger Steggink, O. Carm., *Tiempo y vida de Santa Teresa* (Madrid: Editorial Católica, 1977), 816;822-23; and 68, n. 146.

11 Ana de San Agustín, 72.

12 Ana de San Agustín, 74; "mucha cantidad de demonios y con gran furia començaron a tormentar[la] con muchos y terribles tormentos."

13 Ana de San Agustín, 75.

14 Ana de San Agustín, 74.

15 Teresa of Ávila, *Life,* 32.1 in *Complete Works of Saint Teresa of Jesus,* 1:215- 16; "Parecíame la entrada a manera de un callejón muy largo y estrecho, a manera de horno muy bajo y escuro y angosto; el suelo me pareció de un agua como lodo muy sucio y de pestilencial olor, y muchas sabandijas malas en él; a el cabo estava una concavidad metida en una pared, a manera de un alacena, adonde me vi meter en mucho estrecho." Spanish citations from the works of St. Teresa of Ávila are taken from Santa Teresa de Jesús, *Obras completas,* ed.

Efrén de la Madre de Dios, O.C.D. and Otger Steggink, O. Carm. (Madrid: Editorial Católica, 1972).

[16] Teresa of Ávila, *Life*, 32.2 and 32.3.

[17] Ana de San Agustín, 76, my translation; "al cauo desta profunda estrechura vi en su remate otro çentro mas profundo que era la infernal morada del ynfierno llena de fuego y demonios y çercada de confusion espantable a la uista y temerosisima para mi alma . . . ui que ponçoñosas sauandijas entrauan y salian por los sentidos de aquellas almas dañadas."

[18] Teresa of Ávila, *Life*, 38.1 in *Complete Works of Saint Teresa* of Jesus, 1:267; "Parecíame estar metida en el cielo, y las primeras personas que allá vi, fue a mi padre y madre, y tan grandes cosas—en tan breve espacio . . .—que yo quedé bien fuera de mí."

[19] See *Visionary Life*, 70;98;108, for examples.

[20] Ana de San Agustín, 108-109.

[21] Ana de San Agustín, 115.

[22] Ana de San Agustín, 116.

[23] The two Anas traveled together on the journey to found the house at Villanueva de la Jara and, together, witnessed a rapture by Santa Teresa. Even the saint acknowledged the friendship that existed between her nurse-secretary and Ana de San Agustín in a letter to the latter on 22 May 1581, in *The Letters of Saint Teresa of Jesus*, trans. E. Allison Peers, 2 vols. (London: Sheed and Ward, 1980), 2:837-38.

[24] Ana de San Agustín, 103-104.

[25] Ana de San Agustín, 104; "despues desto cosa de seys u siete años poco mas a menos fue echado de n[uest]ra religión."

[26] Alberto de la Virgen del Carmen, O.C.D., *Historia de la Reforma Teresiana (1562-1962)*(Madrid: Editorial de Espiritualidad, 1968), 72-89; Joachim Smet, O. Carm., *The Carmelites: A History of the Brothers of Our Lady of Mount Carmel,* vol. 2 (Darien, IL: Carmelite Spiritual Center, 1976); and Otilio Rodríguez of the Infant Jesus, O.C.D., *A History of the Teresian Carmel: An Abridgement of Its Origin and Development, 1562-1979* (Rome: Teresianum, n.d.), provide different interpretations of the view concerning the struggle between Doria and Gracián.

[27] Ana de San Agustín, 105; "rebeldía en obedeçer a muchas veçes que los perlados [l]e habian mandado esta mortificaçion de escrivir estas cosas."

[28] Ana de San Agustín, 105-106; "estando actualmente escriviendo en ella me los quemaron sin ber quien."

29   See *Complete Works of Saint Teresa of Jesus,* 2:353, regarding the manuscript of the *Meditaciones sobre el Cantar de los Cantares (Meditations on the Song of Songs).* In the opening lines of the *Camino de perfección (Way of Perfection),* the saint herself invites the confessor to burn the manuscript if he detects any error in it.

30   Ana de San Agustín, 106; "esimida por ser lo último de su probinçialato."

31   Ana de San Agustín, 107.

Blessed Anne of St. Bartholomew

Kieran Kavanaugh, O.C.D.

Institute of Carmelite Studies

The Frenchman Jean de Bretigny (1556-1634) was the first to try to bring the Discalced Carmelite nuns from Spain to France. While in Seville in 1583, he discovered the Teresian Carmel and became a friend of Jerónimo Gracián, who was then provincial. Also getting to know María de San José, the prioress in Seville and dear friend of Teresa, he began speaking to both about the possibility of bringing the Teresian Carmel to France. The Frenchman was invited to present his proposal to the chapter held in October, 1585 in Pastrana. Incidentally, St. John of the Cross was a member of this chapter. The chapter members received De Bretigny's proposal favorably and presented only two conditions: the first was to obtain permission from the king of France; the second was to begin with a foundation of the friars, which would soon be followed by a foundation for the nuns. In a letter signed also by Fray John of the Cross, the provincial and his counselors appointed Jean de Bretigny procurator for a foundation of Carmelites in France. De Bretigny, however, had been in Spain five years. When he returned to France, he found the political situation highly changed, a situation in which it would have in no way been possible to make a foundation of Discalced Carmelite friars at that time. De Bretigny did not lose his love for the Teresian Carmel, though, and in fact translated into French the writings of St. Teresa and published them in three volumes in 1601. Their success was immediate.

France had a kind of fascination with Catholic Spain. Spain had become a living model of a Christianity that the eldest daughter of the

Church had to reconstruct after the damage caused by the Calvinists and the first assaults of the libertines. For some historians Spain remained outside a certain type of Catholic reform after the Protestant reformation, if one understands by Catholic Reformation the struggle against heresy, the missions of the Jesuits in Protestant countries, the extension of the authority of the pope and of the tridentine theology. This concept did not fit Spain well. But if it signifies a new orientation toward an interior Catholicism, on the level of spirituality, Teresa of Ávila participates in this vast movement. She constructed a way of life that would promote unceasing prayer, which she thought was the most important element in the rule of Carmel. But the prayer was centered in friendship with Jesus and she developed her teaching out of her own mystical experience of the evolution of this friendship. Along with this interior life of prayer, she loved the liturgy, its ceremonies, its saints, relics, pilgrimages, statues and paintings, and books for spiritual reading.

Pierre de Bérulle was born in France in 1575. Educated at the Sorbonne, he was ordained in 1599. Refusing all offices, preferring to devote himself entirely to spiritual direction, controversy with the Protestants, and the promotion of reform among the religious communities, he was concerned as well with the education of the clergy. All this led him to found in Paris the French Oratory. He composed many spiritual books, was created cardinal in 1627, and died in Paris in 1629. Innocent X introduced the process for Bérulle's beatification.

Pierre de Bérulle began to work with De Bretigny to bring the Carmelite nuns to France as a part of his idea for reform of the Church in France. His desire was to begin in France with the nuns who knew St. Teresa. They were Anne of Jesus, for whom St. John of the Cross had written his commentary on the *Spiritual Canticle*, and Blessed Anne of St. Bartholomew, a lay sister who traveled with Teresa and served as her secretary and nurse during her later years. I plan to limit myself in this paper for the most part to the relationship between Anne of St. Bartholomew and Pierre de Bérulle.[1]

In 1981 Fr. Julián Urkiza published volume one of his critical edition of the complete works of Blessed Anne of St. Bartholomew. In 1985, the second volume appeared, which consisted of a critical edition of the letters. Anne became a writer by necessity. Her preference was for the menial tasks within the order, the tasks of a lay sister. In her writings she reveals her soul to her confessors and superiors and tells about her mystical life: her visions, locutions, and revelations, her sufferings and joys, her problems and need for light on certain matters. Her desire is always to follow the safe path of Christ and be guided by the light of her confessor and superior. In other writings Anne gives us a first-hand account of the historical events surrounding the beginnings of the Teresian Carmel in Spain, France, and the Spanish Netherlands. To these writings we must add an enormous correspondence of which 650 letters are conserved. The letters are addressed to all peoples in society. The particular qualities of Blessed Anne's personality that stand out in her writings are simplicity, humility, affability, determination, and honesty. With regard to honesty, she could be downright blunt when she thought it was necessary.

If it were not possible to bring Discalced Carmelite friars to France, De Bretigny began to think, then at least Teresa's constitutions could be brought and women in France could learn how to live them. As things developed, Jean de Bretigny ended up bringing three ladies from the upper stratum of French society to Spain to learn Spanish and how to live the Teresian life. Pierre de Bérulle and two other important gentlemen from France joined them. They did not find it easy to convince the Spaniards to allow Spanish nuns to go to France. Their efforts took almost a year.

Many in Spain were not in favor of the nuns' going to France. In her writings Blessed Anne reflects the Spanish Catholic mind of the times, in which Protestants were referred to as heretics. And she tells us that Bérulle had many trials in trying to get permission for the nuns to come to France. People began spreading the rumor that he was a heretic and that he was just trying to get the nuns into France so that he could then trick them into heresy. One priest told Blessed Anne that it wasn't necessary for nuns to go to France among so many heresies since they couldn't preach. She says that everyone in her house was distressed about her going and filled with fear for her since France was so full of heresies. They did all they could to prevent the superiors of the order from giving her permission to make the journey.

Blessed Anne of St. Bartholomew was a Castilian born in a little town of eighty inhabitants called Almendral. She had three brothers and three sisters. When ten years old she lost both her parents in a plague that spread through Spain. In contrast to St. Teresa whose extraordinary mystical experiences began only after many years of prayer, Anne of St. Bartholomew's extraordinary spiritual life had its beginning when she was a child and continued throughout her life. When I speak of extraordinary spiritual or mystical experiences, I am speaking of visions and revelations.

Anne of St. Bartholomew entered St. Joseph's in Ávila in 1570, at the age of twenty-one. She entered as a lay sister, having a very strong constitution with an amazing capacity for hard work. Often times she was so busy during the day that she didn't have time for prayer. She would then devote her time to prayer during the night. When she entered Carmel she did not know how to write. Her brothers had been taught by the local priest to read and write. Anne was taught just enough to be able to learn the catechism. She didn't learn how to write until she had entered Carmel, and she learned from

Teresa herself. After Teresa's death in 1582, Anne of St. Bartholomew exercised great influence as the nun who had known Teresa best.

After many difficulties and much persistence on Bérulle's part, a caravan set out from Spain under the leadership of Bérulle with the Discalced Carmelite nuns destined to make a foundation in Paris. Two of the nuns had been particularly close to Teresa, Anne of Jesus and Anne of St. Bartholomew. Bérulle had promised he would place the nuns under the jurisdiction of the order when a house of Discalced Carmelite friars was founded in France. And this was the condition under which the nuns had come. But as time went on the Spanish nuns began to see that Bérulle had his own plans that would keep them away from the jurisdiction of the friars.

During the rough travel Blessed Anne was most impressed by Bérulle, who had demonstrated much virtue when in Spain and in the midst of the suspicions he had aroused. Now he was showing it again by his manner throughout a very difficult journey. She was in fact more edified by Bérulle and Jean de Bretigny than she was by some of her nun companions. The Frenchmen showed concern for the nuns in the troubles of the journey. She says they were very patient and composed and that they didn't use any of the light banter that makes such long journeys easier to bear.

The caravan arrived in Paris on 15 October 1604. They were well received by the princess of Longueville, Catherine d'Orléans. Bérulle then began to give the first indications that he had his own plans for the Teresian Carmels in France. He had promised to place the nuns under the jurisdiction of the order when a house of Discalced Carmelite friars was founded in France. This was the condition under which the nuns had come. When the king of France, Henry IV, heard that two of the friars had accompanied the group, he sent word asking them to remain and assuring that he would give permission for them to make a foundation. But Bérulle, in hearing of this, got the friars up early in the morning before word could reach them and with gracious words bade them goodbye and sent them on their way. He consoled the nuns by telling them that the promise would be kept.

The first novices represented the higher stratum of society. Blessed Anne says they were all very capable and persevered and later became prioresses, subprioresses, and novice mistresses. With regard to learning French, Blessed Anne never succeeded very well. She was happy to observe silence, happy to be in a foreign land and to serve in the kitchen, refectory, and the rest of the house as though she were a novice.

Her happiness lasted only briefly. Bérulle took the next step in his plan. Impressed by Blessed Anne's simplicity, obedience, and openness, he thought he would get on better with her than he would with the strong-minded Anne of Jesus. Bérulle asked Blessed Anne to become a choir nun and thereby make herself eligible for the office of prioress. This created a crisis for Blessed Anne. She felt a strong aversion toward taking the black veil, the veil of the choir nun in contrast to the white veil of the lay sister. Conversely she recognized the obligation to obey her superior, who now was Bérulle.[2] The administration of the nuns had been placed under the jurisdiction of three priests, Gallemant, Duval, and Bérulle. The latter had told her that he had wanted to make her novice mistress. But Blessed Anne said that she could do that work without taking the black veil. Anne of Jesus for her part was unhappy with Bérulle's wishes and tried to persuade Blessed Anne to refuse, saying that it would go against the spirit of St. Teresa. Blessed Anne could only respond that Teresa herself wanted her to change and take the black veil, but because of Blessed Anne's repugnance toward the idea, she let the matter drop.

Arrangements were then made for the famous Jesuit confessor

of Henry IV, Père Coton, to come and speak to Blessed Anne. She told him the entire story of her affliction. He told her that he would get many people to pray over the matter and that he would do so himself and come back to let her know his opinion. After a novena of prayers and Masses, Father Coton returned and told her that in conscience she was obliged to obey and that he thought he could on the part of God order her under obedience to do so; that he was in fact so ordering her and that she would sin if she chose to do differently. After Father Coton's strong words Blessed Anne resigned herself to what the superiors wanted and received the black veil on 13 January 1605.

Two days later she was on her way to Pontoise, the next foundation in France, where Blessed Anne was to remain as prioress. The day after her arrival, four young French women received the habit, and after two days Mother Anne of Jesus returned to Paris. The Spanish nun from Burgos, Isabel de San Pablo, originally from the Spanish Netherlands, remained as subprioress. She spoke Spanish poorly and French worse. After Isabel fell sick with the quartan fevers, Anne of St. Bartholomew had to take over the recitation of the office in Latin in choir. Anne described her situation in this way: "Since I didn't know how the office should be said in choir, and I found myself there every day alone with the four novices and I didn't know the language, I was the most embarrassed woman in the world and so cast down that I didn't think anything could have been more humbling for me. I felt so incapable that I didn't know myself."[3] She said that the only time she had ever felt so afflicted was when St. Teresa died. She tells us, though, that the French nuns read Latin very well (in fact, as though they had doctorates) and that they had to teach her. Blessed Anne was always very impressed by the French nuns and thought they made excellent Carmelites. To this Spanish nun they seemed "more like angels than creatures."

Before the year was out, Bérulle arranged to bring Blessed Anne back to Paris. Anne of Jesus was now threatening to return to Spain and had written to the Father General from Dijon, where she had just made a foundation, to come for her and her two companions from Salamanca and to take them back to Spain. They were not satisfied with the way things were proceeding under Bérulle. Anne of Jesus wrote to Blessed Anne asking her if she would like to return to Spain with them. Blessed Anne responded that she thought the foundations in France were the work of God and that if she went back it would be like abandoning the cross.[4]

The people in Pontoise had quickly grown attached to Blessed Anne. When word got around that Bérulle wanted her back in Paris, they took up their arms to prevent such a thing from happening. Bérulle's agents had to disguise Blessed Anne in a man's hat and coat and sneak her out in the middle of the night. While Blessed Anne had been in Pontoise, she continued to write to Bérulle as her superior with great simplicity and openness, informing him of everything and manifesting to him the state of her soul. Bérulle thought that he could carry out his plan in Paris very well with the help of this simple, humble, and docile Carmelite. In Paris Blessed Anne found many novices who all received her well. Life in Paris went on peacefully for close to a year, and Anne's relationship with the novices was especially satisfying to her. She was amazed by their innocence, simplicity, openness, and affability toward her. For her part, she felt limited and embarrassed, for she still was unable to read the breviary.

She had also come to understand the need of adapting to the temperaments of the French nuns. She writes of them:

These souls are docile in matters of virtue and they are guided better by gentleness and sisterly love, and one can show them their faults and they take it well. The conditions in our country are different, for the superiors act with greater superiority and make themselves feared through strictness rather than act with gentleness…And certainly I can do this better because it is more in conformity with Jesus Christ who if we consider it acted with his disciples as a brother and companion.[5]

But then Bérulle started to move in, to take greater control, and Blessed Anne's difficulties with him began. He was afraid that if the French nuns became too attached to Blessed Anne, they would side with her should the friars came to France and would place themselves under the obedience of the order. The French nuns were encouraged not to discuss their spiritual lives with Blessed Anne. They were told that she was a foreigner and Spanish and that if the friars came they would treat the nuns cruelly. Blessed Anne noticed little by little that the nuns stopped speaking with her on any serious level.

As Anne's confessor, Bérulle counseled that she not try to teach the nuns by words but only by patience. This put Anne into a difficult situation, for Bérulle was insisting that she be prioress in name only and not according to the idea that Teresa had wanted for her prioresses. Blessed Anne then asked for an official visitation of the order. Bérulle reasoned that since there were no friars of the order in France, the visitation could be made by the Carthusians. But he then informed the Carthusians that they could not do or undo anything without his say in the matter. The Carthusians answered that with such restrictions there would be no point in their making a visitation.[6] Bérulle then arranged for the nuns to be governed by the opinions of the noted Madame Acarie and Madame Marillac. Madame Acarie told Blessed Anne about the nuns who were doing well and those who did not have the right spirit. She also told Blessed Anne that she must obey Bérulle.[7]

At this time Blessed Anne kept asking Bérulle if she could have another confessor. But he refused and said that God was showing him her sins. She began to suffer a dark night, a true purgatory day and night in which she had doubts about her salvation. She says explicitly "my soul was as in a dark night." "And God so hid from me that my soul seemed never to have known him, and it experienced so many fears it seemed to be without faith and without anyone to speak to about it."[8]

At this time Anne of Jesus passed through Paris on her way to the Spanish Netherlands to make a foundation in Brussels. Catherine of Orléans, the princess of Longueville, who was able to live in the monastery because she was the patron of the foundation, urged Anne of Jesus to take Blessed Anne with her on account of the difficulties with Bérulle. But Blessed Anne refused, thinking that God still wanted her to remain in France. Finally Blessed Anne convinced Bérulle to have an election and let someone else be prioress so that she could be free of responsibility for the way things were going. He agreed and the noted Madeleine de St. Joseph was elected prioress of the Carmel in Paris on 20 April 1608. Blessed Anne was pleased with the choice. Madeleine was a spiritual daughter of Bérulle's. She sang his praises and assimilated his doctrine, becoming a faithful echo of it to the Carmelite nuns in France. But she also had influence on Bérulle in some of his thinking. Her cause was introduced in 1645 and the heroicity of her virtues declared in 1789.

Blessed Anne's freedom did not last long. In May Bérulle decided to send her to make a foundation in Tours. At first she was glad to get away, but soon discovered that Bérulle managed to stay close to her. A subprioress, who had been instructed to watch her carefully and to keep Bérulle informed, dutifully informed him that Blessed Anne had a portress in whom she greatly confided. Bérulle then gave orders for a change and arranged that any letter going to or coming from Spain be intercepted and sent to him. Blessed Anne behaved as though not aware of this and continued writing about her desire to see the friars come to France.

After her term as prioress in Tours, Blessed Anne petitioned to return to Paris, since a group of friars from the Italian congregation (led by the Spaniard Thomas of Jesus) had arrived in May,1610 with the intention of making foundations in France and the Netherlands. Two of the friars who were French made the foundation in Paris; the others continued on to the Netherlands.[9] Blessed Anne freely told Bérulle of her desire to return to the obedience of the order. He and his followers were saddened and did not want her to make this change. Anne gives her own interpretation of their desire to keep her in France: "[t]hey were not pleased with me nor did they want me for any reason but their own vanity, so that they could tell everybody that Holy Mother's companion got along well under their government and wants to stay with them."[10]

After the Discalced Carmelite friars arrived in Paris, Bérulle was able to obtain a bull from Rome appointing him visitator for life for the Carmelite nuns in France.[11] The French Oratory, which he had founded, and the French Carmelite nuns had a juridical structure strongly centralized in Bérulle's hands. He was the general superior of the Oratory and the official visitator for the nuns in France. He did not limit himself just to juridical aspects, forming the nuns in his spirit, which was heavily influenced by Neo-platonic mysticism, deeply rooted in Pseudo-Dionysius the Areopagite. When Bérulle died 1 October 1629, there were forty-three Carmels in France under his authority. A couple of years later the Congregation of the Oratory requested that the Holy See free them from the obligation of jurisdiction over the Carmelite nuns. The Carmelite nuns in France were then placed under the jurisdiction of the nuncio and eventually under that of their bishops.

Blessed Anne of St. Bartholomew made the following assessment of Bérulle: "I hold that because Msgr. Bérulle went back on his promise to the superiors of the order and to the Spanish nuncio, God now permits him to fall into errors and away from the virtuous beginning. He gets himself caught in so many snares and everybody else along with him."[12]

---

[1]   The information in this paper comes primarily from Blessed Anne of St. Bartholomew's two autobiographies and her *Defensa de la herencia teresiana* (Defense of the Teresian Heritage). These texts may be found in *Obras completas de la Beata Ana de San Bartolomé*, ed. Julián Urkiza, 2 vols. (Rome: Teresianum, 1981), vol 1. Although her account becomes unfavorable toward Bérulle as events unfold, Blessed Anne certainly tried much harder to get along with him than did Anne of Jesus.

[2]   Jurisdiction of the Carmelite nuns in France was confined to three priests: Jacques Gallemant, André Duval, and Pierre de Bérulle. The temporal care was entrusted to these three administrators. But their power also extended to spiritual matters. They could issue decrees concerning administration, persons, and spiritual and temporal things and goods. See the bull *In supremo,* 13 November 1603.

[3]   Ana de San Bartolomé, *Noticias sobre los origines del carmelo teresiano en Francia,* in *Obras completas,* 1:170-89, at 182.

[4]   She tells us that the others became angry with her since they were already annoyed over another matter. This concerned a bone of contention between Anne of Jesus and Bérulle. Bérulle had wanted Anne of Jesus to accept a young woman who, in Blessed Anne's words, had been a "heretic." Anne of Jesus refused adamantly despite Bérulle's insistence. Then in Pontoise Blessed Anne received this woman. She writes: "Mother Anne [of Jesus] wrote to me rudely that I had gone against my constitutions and against the laws of Spain and wondered if I knew that it was forbidden for the order to receive persons who had been heretics. I answered that I thought we had come to help them and show charity toward them in every way we could. But since this didn't bring quiet I wrote to Father General about the matter."

In his answer the general mentioned that he had discussed the case with the best doctors at the University of Alcalá and that they told him it would be ignorant to think they went to this country for the Catholics alone, but they went to help those who were outside Catholicism so that they would return to the faith. See Ana de San Bartolomé, *Defensa de la herencia teresiana,* in *Obras completas,* 1:378-421, at 407.

5   Ana de San Bartolomé, *Noticias,* 185-186.

6   Until the Discalced Carmelite friars came to France the Prior General of the Carthusians had the right to make visitations.

7   Barbe Acarie (Avrillot)(1566-1618) played an important role in bringing the Carmelite nuns to France. She gathered around herself devout young women whom she trained in the spiritual life and who later entered the French Carmel. After her husband's death, she entered the Carmel of Amiens as a lay sister, taking the name Marie of the Incarnation. She died in Pontoise 18 April 1618 and was beatified 25 April 1791.

8   Ana de San Bartolomé, *Autobiografía A,* in *Obras completas,* 1:278-377, at 346-349.

9   Denys of the Mother of God and Bernard of St. Joseph were two Frenchmen from the monastery of St. Anne's in Genoa. They took over the foundation in Paris. But Denys had a combative temperament. He could be hateful and vulnerable and became an implacable adversary of Bérulle's.

10   Ana de San Bartolomé, *Autobiografía A,* 361.

11   *Cum Pridem,* 17 April 1614. The friars who headed for the Netherlands insisted that Bérulle allow Blessed Anne to go with them. He tried to get her to promise obedience to him, but she refused, having always wanted from the beginning to remain under the obedience of the order. Finally the Frenchman gave in and allowed her to go.

12   Ana de San Bartolomé, *Defensa,* 402.

Taking Teresian Authority to the Front Lines: Ana de San Bartolomé and Ana de Jesús in Art of the Spanish Netherlands

Christopher C. Wilson
The Holton-Arms School
Institutum Carmelitanum

Within early modern Catholicism one primary aim of the picture was to champion cults of sanctity. Religious orders and individuals promoted devotion to certain deceased nuns, for example, by commissioning biographical narrative paintings, copies of portraits, and engravings of adored female subjects. Such representations functioned like the printed hagiography: they were intended to convince the viewer of the nun's sanctity and help elevate her to the status of religious celebrity, thereby fueling momentum toward canonization. This essay concentrates on seventeenth-century representations of two Discalced Carmelite nuns closest to St. Teresa of Ávila, Ana de San Bartolomé (1549-1626) and Ana de Jesús (1545-1621), exploring how artistic portrayals served the cults—or, to put it more precisely, the rival cults—of each, while also considering how their iconography reflected changes within the expanding Carmelite reform, including its increased politicization. Though both women were born in Spain, they spent the final decades of their lives in the Spanish Netherlands, where iconographic cults sprang up soon after their deaths. The paintings, prints, and drawings that I will investigate are all Flemish in origin, often by unidentified artists, most of which I photographed during recent visits to Discalced Carmelite convents. They now are preserved in convent archives but were assigned more public functions at the time of their creation: paintings might have been displayed in convent church interiors and engravings were given or sold to increase devotion among the general population. These works have received little, if any, attention in scholarship, yet they reveal much about the aspirations and tensions within an order during a time of remarkable growth and transition.[1]

Before examining specific images, I will first review the key events of the two Anas' lives. Ana de San Bartolomé was born in 1549 in the Castilian village of El Almendral to a family of landowning farmers.[2] Her parents died when she was ten years old, leaving her to be raised by her siblings. As a teenager, she declares in her autobiographical writings, she had a vision in which the Virgin told her she would become a nun, and another in which she saw the convent and nuns of St. Joseph's, the first foundation made by Teresa in the city of Ávila.[3] Despite opposition from her family, she took the veil as a lay sister there in 1570. In 1577 Teresa chose Ana as her personal assistant. The ailing foundress needed not only a nurse, but also a secretary to help with her voluminous correspondence. As a child, Ana had acquired only a rudimentary ability to read in the vernacular. One of the miracles cited during Teresa's beatification and canonization proceedings was that she miraculously gave Ana the ability to write in a single afternoon, by presenting her with two lines of her own handwriting from which to learn.[4]

During the last five years of Teresa's life Ana was her inseparable companion, traveling with her and assisting in her last four convent foundations. Teresa died in Ana's arms in 1582, at the Discalced Carmelite convent in Alba de Tormes. In 1604, as Kieran Kavanaugh explains in his essay in this volume, she was among the group of nuns chosen to accompany Ana de Jesús on the expedition to France, where she took the black veil as a choir nun. She assisted in the foundation of French Discalced Carmelite convents and served as prioress at

Pontoise, Paris, and Tours. Her rise to the position of founder and prioress was remarkable for a woman of the peasant class who, in Spain, had been a lay sister. She founded a convent at Antwerp in 1612, where she remained until her death in 1626.

By the last years of her life Ana had attained the status of local celebrity. Large numbers of sick came to the Antwerp convent, seeking water that she had blessed. Miracles began to be attributed to her soon after her death, including Marie de Medici's testimony that Ana's mantle cured her of a severe fever in 1633. Ana's first biographer, Crisóstomo Enríquez, asserts that by the time of his writing (1632) the bishops had approved over 150 miracles.[5] In 1735 Pope Clement XII declared the heroicity of her virtues. She was beatified by Benedict XV in 1917.

Ana de Jesús was another giant of Teresa's reform. Her leadership was sought after, extolled and restricted at various periods of her life.[6] Ana was born in 1545 in Medina del Campo to a Castilian hidalgo family of modest prosperity. She lived as a penitent under Jesuit spiritual direction before entering the Convent of St. Joseph in Ávila at the age of twenty-five, subsequently making her profession at Salamanca in 1571, where she first met Teresa. The saint installed Ana as prioress of the new foundation at Beas in 1575. It was there that Ana developed a close friendship with John of the Cross, who served as her confessor, and it was to her that he would dedicate his commentary on the *Spiritual Canticle*.[7] From Beas she went to Granada, founding a convent in 1582 under Teresa's direction via letters, and in 1586 made the long-anticipated foundation in Madrid. While in the capital she forged links with the Spanish court through Empress Maria of Austria, sister of Philip II, and recruited Luis de León to edit the first published edition of Teresa's writtten works (1588). After falling out of favor with Nicolás Doria, Provincial of the Discalced, for disputing his changes to the Teresian constitutions, she was stripped of her authority within the order and imprisoned in her cell for three years. After Doria's death she was elected prioress at Salamanca in 1596, where she gathered strength for the next momentous chapter, that of carrying the reform to France and eventually Flanders. A possible attraction of this venture was that it gave her the opportunity to distance herself from those in Spain who saw her as a troublemaking rebel, taking on instead the identity of missionary-like convent founder in regions that had been affected by the spread of Protestantism. Leading a group of five nuns, including Ana de San Bartolomé, she made a foundation at Paris in 1604. After establishing houses at Pontoise (with Ana de San Bartolomé) and Dijon, she went to Flanders, founding a Carmel in Brussels in 1607 under the patronage of the Archdukes Albert and Isabella, and later at Leuven and Mons. In 1614 she was struck by a chronic illness that brought on excruciating physical symptoms of paralysis, sciatica, tumors, and night sweats. She died in Brussels in 1621. Though there was immediate movement for her beatification, her cult gradually dissipated and she was not declared Venerable until1878.

The Two Anas as Friends of God from Childhood

Here we have women from two classes—Ana de Jesús aristocratic in comparison with Ana de San Bartolomé's peasant origins—whose difference in status continued within the convent: Ana de Jesús, trained by a Jesuit, entered as a choir nun, while Ana de San Bartolomé, who professed with only a rudimentary ability to read in the vernacular, remained a lay sister until her move to Paris. Teresa entrusted Ana de Jesús with important administrative responsibilities, while Ana de San Bartolomé's activities centered on serving the saint's physical needs and writing letters for her. Even today the nuns

of Ana de Jesús' community in Brussels point out contrasts between
the two, asserting that their Ana's intellect and refined manners made
her a more suitable leader for the transplantation of Carmel to France
and for the prickly negotiations with French superior Pierre de
Bérulle.[8] Yet visual representations of the two nuns do show similarities, since they conform to the hagiographic paradigm in art and literature of presenting the subject as a friend of God from childhood, a
motif that also exists in the first chapter of Teresa's *Vida,* where she
describes her and her brother's fascination with reading lives of the
saints and their building of makeshift hermitages.

In the Discalced Carmelite convent of Madrid is a series of
twelve painted miniatures on paper, created in Flanders, probably in
the 1640s.[9] They illustrate episodes recounted in Ana de San
Bartolomé's autobiography. One shows her as a young shepherdess,
guarding her family's flock while accompanied by the Christ Child in
an idyllic pastoral setting (Figure 1). The subject is repeated in a draw-
ing in the convent archives of the Antwerp Carmel, part of a series
visualizing Ana's life that formed the basis for an eventual print cycle
(Figure 2).[10] Both compositions show her, like the young Teresa, as
called by God from birth to a life of intimacy with him. Similarly, portrayals of the young Ana de Jesús present her as the recipient of divine
favors. In the Brussels Carmel is a mid-seventeenth-century canvas
representing her miraculous childhood cure by the Virgin (Figure 3),
one in a series of narrative scenes of Ana's life (no artist's signature is
visible).[11] According to biographers she was born deaf and mute. Her
family prayed for a cure, and at the age of seven she spontaneously
said aloud the "Ave Maria."[12] The painting depicts a surprised Ana
pointing to her mouth and ears, her eyes fixed on a statue of the Virgin
and Child.

Both Anas are depicted as attractive young women rejecting

suitors in favor of Christ. One of the drawings at the Antwerp Carmel situates Ana de San Bartolomé within a party setting with musicians and dancing (Figure 4). Though a gentleman reaches out toward her, she instead gazes upward, where an apparition of the wounded Christ, crowned with thorns, demands her attention. The image draws upon Ana's autobiography, in which she describes her brothers' insistence that she wed, and her own resolution that she would only marry if a just man appeared who was virtuous and beautiful; since earthly men seemed ugly, only Christ fit her criteria and revealed himself as her true spouse.[13] A painting in the Brussels Carmel similarly shows Ana de Jesús in a moment of spiritual awakening that leads her to resist occasions for romantic attention (Figure 5). In the foreground an elegantly dressed Ana cuts off her hair and prepares to put on a black, habit-like garment, a scene that echoes contemporary representations of the conversion of the Magdalen. In the background is a garden banquet, where guests awaiting Ana's arrival register shock at seeing the newly formed penitent emerge from the house. Her family's plans to marry her are thereby foiled.[14] All these images perform the same function: they indicate to the viewer that each Ana took on a nun-like life of asceticism as bride of Christ even before entering the convent.

The Anas as Teresa's Successors

While the images just discussed present the two Anas as friends of God from childhood, more loaded with institutional implications are those that proclaim them as friends of Teresa, each shaped by the Founding Mother as a deserving guardian of her heritage. Ana de San Bartolomé's authority rested on her physical proximity to the saint, whom she served as traveling companion, secretary, and nurse. In one of the Flemish miniatures now in Madrid (Figure 6), the two are placed in a landscape before a mound, a reference to Mount Carmel.

Teresa places her hand upon the head of the kneeling Ana, as if blessing her protégée. Accompanying the miniature is a poem: "In the mirror of Teresa/She saw herself, and took counsel/She was Teresa's
image, and not a mere sketch/Since her virtue revealed it."[15] The painting and poem set up the idea that, because Ana was directly trained by
Teresa and enjoyed unparalleled intimacy with her, she was her spiritual heir, a daughter molded in the Mother's image. Teresa died in Ana
de San Bartolomé's arms in 1582, sealing the latter's reputation as a
living relic of the saint. Believing herself to be the transmitter of
Teresa's will—a role confirmed by posthumous visits from Teresa,
according to Ana's autobiographical texts—she asserted enormous
authority. Another painted miniature in the same Madrid series boldly
conveys the notion of the passing of Teresa's authority to Ana (Figure
7). In a posthumous apparition, Teresa descends from heaven to bless
the kneeling nun. The accompanying poem explains that just as Elijah
passed on a double portion of his spirit to Elisha, Teresa did the same
for Ana: "The Reformer, another Elijah/In showing her wish/To her
daughter, as to Elisha/Improves her in spirit."[16]

A seventeenth-century painting in the Brussels Carmel , however, makes a case for the transfer of Teresian authority to Ana de Jesús,
who receives a copy of the Discalced Carmelite constitutions from the
seated saint (Figure 8). Much of Ana's efforts and a good deal of her
suffering surrounded her adamant resistance to proposed revisions to
the Teresian constitutions. As this painting contends, her authority
rested on direct continuity of Teresa's administrative command,
beginning during the saint's life when Ana was appointed prioress at
Beas and was later sent to make the foundation at Granada in Teresa's
absence. Early biographers, such as Ange Manrique in his 1639 publication, attributed statements to Teresa about Ana's senior position
within the reform: "Ana does all the work and I get the credit," and

"They call me foundress, but it is Ana de Jesús who deserves the title."[17] Thus, while images of the two Anas contain similarities, showing them as friends of God and trusted companions of Teresa, they also stress the exceptionalism of each as Teresa's favored heir.

Ana Factions

Such images of the two Anas must be viewed, at least in part, against the backdrop of competition that existed between them and their admirers. I propose that each nun's iconography reflects not only her own self-identification as the protector of Teresa's spiritual heritage, but also reveals the attempt by rival cults to promote the case for each nun's sanctity in the decades after her death through the use of strategic representations. Antagonism between the two women was rooted in a 1590 conflict known as "the nuns' revolt." When Nicolás Doria proposed changes in monastic governance and sought to alter the Teresian constitutions, Ana de Jesús led a group of rebel nuns and petitioned the pope to forbid changes to the primitive constitutions drafted by the Founding Mother. Ana de San Bartolomé, however, sided with Doria, convinced that Teresa would have endorsed major points of his proposed reform.

Tensions flared up again in 1605, when Ana de Jesús, then prioress in Paris, rejected an English postulant who had converted from Protestantism. In defiant response Ana de San Bartolomé accepted the English novice at her convent in Pontoise. In a letter to Bérulle regarding this issue Ana de Jesús condescendingly dismisses the other Ana's judgment:

> As for Mother Ana de San Bartolomé, she has had no occasion up to the present of knowing what it means to make or abrogate a point of Rule or of the Constitutions. If our Holy Mother, four

or five years before her death, had her constantly with her, it was not to help in business, but only to dress and undress her and to help her to write letters, for her Reverence had broken her arm and the choir nuns could not always be with her.[18]

Ana de San Bartolomé, in her text *Defense of the Teresian Legacy (Defensa de la herencia teresiana),* dated by Urkiza to 1621, offers her own spin on the recently-deceased Ana de Jesús:

...it seems they want to make more of [her] than our Holy Mother, and this I cannot endure, since she is far from deserving canonization...Mother Ana [de Jesús] was not with the Saint but two or three months in Salamanca and after some years she [the saint] carried her to a new foundation at Veas and left her there, so that they never saw each other again. And through letters our Holy Mother commanded her to go to Granada...and well I know that she was unhappy with how Ana did things there...and what is least to the credit of Mother Ana is that in her life she wanted to be head of everything, and this is not high praise for a subordinate.[19]

In these two excerpts, each Ana undermines the other's claim to authority: if Ana de San Bartolomé was Teresa's constant companion, she was more servant than trusted collaborator; and though Ana de Jesús held positions of administrative leadership, she was too independent-minded and bossy.

Rivalry between the two was assimilated and maintained by protégée nuns of each: Beatriz de la Concepción (1569-1643), confidante to Ana de Jesús and prioress of the Brussels Carmel after her death, energetically sought her friend's beatification. Leonor de San

Bernardo (1577-1639) fulfilled this same role for Ana de San Bartolomé. One of the original nuns of the Antwerp community, she founded two Flemish convents.[20] These women, and the communities of nuns around them, helped to fuel iconographic presentation of the privileged status of each Ana.

It is within the context of the effort to aggrandize the posthumous reputation of each nun that we can situate two prints: one example, a seventeenth-century Flemish engraving by P. Roland van Overstraeten, shows John of the Cross, Teresa, and Ana de Jesús together as the reform's earthly Trinity—Teresa the founder, John and Ana collaborators in propagating the order. Since the inscription refers to John as Venerable, the image must date before his beatification in 1675, at a time when hopes for Ana's own beatification were high (the version illustrated here, as Figure 9, is a nineteenth-century copy engraved by P.I. Arenezen)[21]. But another engraving (Figure 10), by the Antwerp artist Jean Baptiste Barbé (1578-1649), focuses instead on the inseparability of Teresa and Ana de San Bartolomé; an angel draws them together, like spiritual twins, as they gaze up toward the Holy Trinity.[22]

I suggest that a subtle reminder of tensions between the two Anas can be detected in representations of Teresa's death. In one of the Madrid miniatures (Figure 11), Ana de San Bartolomé holds the dying Teresa in her arms as she describes in her autobiography.[23] Similarly, one in the series of drawings in the Antwerp Carmel (Figure 12) shows her supporting Teresa's head, with Christ, the Virgin, and Francis of Assisi standing beside the bed. Ana's physical proximity to Teresa at the moment of her death—the fact that she was holding the dying saint as Teresa drew her last breath—gave her a unique position among the other nuns. It was one of the defining moments of her life and iconography. Yet in a 1613 engraving produced in Antwerp

(Figure 13), one in a widely-circulated series of Teresa's life by Adriaen Collaert and Cornelis Galle, Ana is eliminated from the scene. It shows Teresa on her deathbed, surrounded by Christ, the Virgin, St. Joseph, and angels, but no attendant nun. Interestingly, and perhaps not coincidentally, this print series was produced at the request of Ana de Jesús, who presumably discussed the choice of subjects with the engravers.[24]

Troops in the Church Militant

If each Ana claimed a unique identity as the guardian of Teresa's legacy, they were united in the common purpose of bolstering the Catholic Church in places where it had been threatened by the rapid spread of Protestantism. Historian Concha Torres Sánchez has called attention to the political implications of the Discalced Carmelite expansion into France and Flanders, arguing that the Spanish nuns were utilized as an instrument of power.[25] French elites such as Barbe Acarie and Princess Catherine d'Orléans de Longueville, with her connection to the court of Henry IV, were protagonists in bringing the two Anas from Spain. These aristocratic women recognized the necessity of the importation of Teresa's own companions for the successful cultivation of the Carmelite reform, and by extension, of the larger Catholic revival, in French society. The two Anas' ultimate destination, Flanders, was the Hapsburg Catholic Empire's northern frontier, perilously close to rebellious Protestant provinces of the northern Netherlands. The Spanish monarch faced the ongoing task of fortifying it as a bulwark of Catholicism and of reinforcing its ties with Spain. Philip II had ceded government of the region to his daughter, Isabella Clara Eugenia and Albert of Austria, son of Empress Maria who had been Ana de Jesús' admirer in Madrid. The Archdukes were aware of the strategic value of bringing Spanish nuns imbued with the

Teresian spirit to the region, perceiving it as a key component in their Counter-Reformation agenda. It is significant that they situated the Carmel of Brussels, of which Ana de Jesús was prioress, next to the royal palace, a demonstration of the "pious unity between court and convent."[26] Carmelite communities attracted daughters of the most influential members of the Hispano-Flemish population, thereby reinforcing the desired societal mixture of imported Spanish Catholicism and Flemish economic prosperity. Set up in urban centers, convents became focal points of local piety. The two Anas, then, were agents of the Spanish crown and of the Counter-Reformation Church.

Portrayals of the two assert their identities as female conquistadors who used their inherited Teresian authority to fortify the Church in its geographic areas of most intense need. A seventeenth-century painting of Ana de Jesús in the Brussels Carmel (Figure 14) shows her in prayer, gazing up toward the Virgin, who shelters Carmelite nuns and friars beneath her mantle. A significant feature of this composition is the inclusion of heraldic shields, representing Spain, France, and Flanders, that surround Ana. Here she assumes the role of foreign ambassador, a divinely appointed diplomat who buttressed Catholicism in three realms and found devotees among the royalty and powerful elites of each. If she served the Church and crown through astute founding of convents in three disparate regions, Ana de San Bartolomé was represented as having done so through prayer. One of the Madrid miniatures (Figure 15) places her in a soldierly role, depicting the two occasions when she was credited with rescuing the city of Antwerp from invasion by Protestant troops. In 1622, Maurice of Nassau, Prince of Orange, led an army with the intention of taking the city. But a storm arose, sinking his ships and thwarting the attack. Ana says that she participated in this drama from the confines of her convent cell: "That night, without knowing of the treachery of our enemies, I was struck at about midnight with a great fear and I began to pray, my arms extended toward heaven, and with great fervor."[27] Her arms became tired, but God commanded her to keep them raised. Ana, like Moses with his upraised arms during the battle against Amalek and his troops (Exod. 17:9-13), stayed that way until daybreak and defended the city. The miniature shows Ana kneeling in her cell, arms raised in prayer, with a crucifix, book, and an instrument of penance on the table in front of her. Inscribed on rays of light, pouring into her cell from heaven, are the words *"Ruega mas mas"* (Pray more, more). Through a window is seen the city of Antwerp, in the midst of the storm that destroyed the enemy's ships. The accompanying poem reads: "God, liking her prayer,/Through which he has her accomplish more,/Wanting to free Antwerp/In an imperiled state."[28]

In its portrayal of Ana as a warrior for Christ, this image can be related to one of the prints in Jean Terrier's emblem book glorifying Isabella Clara Eugenia, published in 1635, the subject of a recent study by Cordula van Wyhe (Figure 16).[29] The composition shows a battlefield in which three squadrons of angelic virgins and nuns fight an army of demons. The Virgin stands in the center of the field while Isabella, dressed in the Franciscan habit, leads an army of nuns holding rosaries. Text accompanying the image characterizes the fight not only as a spiritual struggle against vice, but also as a political clash. Isabella and her nuns are fighting the Protestants, chasing away the enemies of the Catholic Church and of the Hapsburg Netherlands. The Franciscan nuns in the image refer to female religious who lived under the Infanta's patronage. Former ladies-in-waiting who entered convents after completing their education at court were regarded as elite members of the Archducal family, and they often chose religious communities under Isabella and Albert's patronage, such as the reformed order of the Poor Clare Colletines in Ghent and, of course, the

Discalced Carmelites in Brussels and Antwerp.[30] Ana de San Bartolomé was certainly regarded as one of the generals in Isabella's army. Seventeenth-century nun Clara de la Cruz quoted Isabella as saying that she feared nothing for Antwerp, since Ana, its saintly protector, would defend the city from attack.[31]

In the archives of the Antwerp Carmel is a seventeenth-century engraving (Figure 17), with which I will conclude, that equates Ana de San Bartolomé's favored status with the territorial expansion of Catholicism. She stands in prayer silhouetted against a map of the Netherlands. Christ crowned with thorns hovers above her, as if displaying the Netherlandish landscape for her contemplation. The inscriptions contain his words to Ana: "Behold all of Holland…I am ready to give this to you" *(Ecce tota Hollandia…hanc tibi dare paratus sum).* Ana's mission, as depicted here, is geographic conquest for Christ and his Church. Just as Ana de Jesús is depicted in the Brussels painting as a unifier of realms, Ana de San Bartolomé is presented here as a leader on the front lines of the Church Militant. Interestingly, this must be the same print described in the writings of seventeenth-century French Ursuline nun Marie of the Incarnation (1599-1672), who traveled to Canada to spread the faith among Native Americans through the founding of a convent school. To encourage her mission, she says, a priest

> …sent me a picture of Mother Ana de Saint-Barthélemy, a Spaniard, in which Our Lord was depicted with his hand pointing to Flanders, inviting her to go serve him there where heresy was causing such ruin. 'I'm sending you this picture,' he wrote 'to urge you to go to serve God in New France'…this was like a spur which activated still more powerfully the fire for the salvation of souls which consumed me.[32]

As Marie's words indicate, the constructed identity of the two Anas as warriors in God's army, chosen from childhood and trained by Teresa, inspired other female "heirs," thereby preserving one strand of Teresian feminism: the saint's insistence on women's usefulness to the Church in a time of crisis. It was in the defense of this apostolic desire to serve that Teresa's daughters stood on common ground both during their lifetimes and, posthumously, in images and texts that argued for their sanctity.

---

[1] I am grateful to the communities of Discalced Carmelite nuns in Madrid, Brussels, and Antwerp, who have been unfailingly supportive of my Teresian studies and have kindly given me access to their archives and collections of art. On Carmelite iconography in the Spanish Netherlands, see Cécile Emond, *L'Iconographie Carmélitaine dans les anciens Pays-Bays méridionaux* (Brussels: Palais des Académies, 1961), and *Teresa de Jesús: Cataloog Tentoonstelling,* exh. cat. (Ghent: Carmelitana, 1982).

[2] For studies of the life and writings of Ana de San Bartolomé, see *Obras completas de la Beata Ana de San Bartolomé,* ed. Julián Urkiza, O.C.D., 2 vols. (Rome: Teresianum, 1981, 1985), 1:53*-205*, cited hereafter as OCASB; Silverio de Santa Teresa,O.C.D., *Historia del Carmen Descalzo en España, Portugal y America,* 15 vols. (Burgos: El Monte Carmelo, 1935-), 8:518-60; Electa Arenal and Stacey Schlau, *Untold Sisters: Hispanic Nuns in Their Own Works,* with translations by Amanda Powell (Albuquerque: University of New Mexico Press, 1989), 21-27 and 30-36; Barbara Mujica, *Women Writers of Early Modern Spain: Sophia's Daughters* (New Haven and London: Yale University Press, 2004), 68-90; Winifred Nevin, *Heirs of St. Teresa of Ávila* (Milwaukee: Bruce, 1959); and Alison Weber, "The Partial Feminism of Ana de San Bartolomé," in *Recovering Spain's Feminist Tradition,* ed. Lisa Vollendorf (New York: The Modern Language Association of America, 2001), 69-87.

[3] Ana de San Bartolomé, *Autobiografía A,* in OCASB, 1:285 and 1:286-87.

[4] See Ana de San Bartolomé's 1595 deposition in *Procesos de beatificación y canonización de Santa Teresa de Jesús,* ed. Silverio de Santa Teresa, O.C.D. (Burgos: Monte Carmelo, 1934), 1:173.

[5] *Historia del Carmen Descalzo,* 8:559. Marie de Medici's declaration is

included in English translation in *Autobiography of the Blessed Mother Anne of Saint Bartholomew,* translated by a religious of the Carmel of St. Louis (St. Louis: 1916), 125-27.

6   For information on Ana de Jesús, see Nevin; Ildefonso Moriones, O.C.D., *Ana de Jesús y la herencia teresiana: Humanismo cristiano o rigor primitivo?* (Rome: Teresianum, 1968); P. Servais, O.C.D., *La Vénérable Ana de Jésus,coadjutrice de Sainte Thérèse et fondatrice du Carmel en France et en Belgique* (Namur: Picard-Balon, 1907); Louis van den Bossche, *Ana de Jésus, coadjutrice de Sainte Thérèse d'Ávila* (Bruges: Desclée de Brouwer, 1958); Marie-Ana de Jésus, *Ana de Jésus, fondatrice du Carmel en France et en Belgique* (France: Éditions du Lion de Juda, 1988); A Sister of Notre Dame de Namur, *Life of the Venerable Ana de Jesús, Companion of St. Teresa of Ávila* (London: Sands, 1932); and Concha Torres Sánchez, *La clausura imposible: Conventualismo femenino y expansión contrarreformista* (Madrid: Al-Mudayna, 2000), 25-32.

7   For more on this relationship see María Pilar Manero Sorrolla, "Ana de Jesús y Juan de la Cruz: Perfil de una relación a examen," *Boletín de la Biblioteca de Menendez Pelayo* 70 (1994): 5-53.

8   This point was made during my conversations with the Discalced Carmelite nuns in Brussels in January, 2004.

9   The miniatures are discussed in Christopher C. Wilson, "A Heroic Successor to St. Teresa of Ávila: Painted Miniatures of Ana de San Bartolomé," *Carmelus* 50 (2003): 129-47. They are bound within a volume containing one of Ana de San Bartolomé's autograph manuscripts, a treatise on the silence, love, and other virtues modeled by Christ, the Virgin Mary, St. Joseph, St. John the Baptist, and contemporary saints (especially Teresa), dated by Urkiza to1618-1622, when she was living in Antwerp (OCASB, 1:659-683). Inserted before the treatise are pages bearing a statement in Spanish by Juan de la Madre de Dios, the Discalced Carmelite Provincial of Flanders and confessor to Ana, signed in Antwerp in 1648, attesting to the authenticity of Ana's handwritten manuscript; and a second testament to the same effect, in French, signed by six of the Discalced Carmelite nuns who lived with Ana at the Antwerp convent. These contents suggest that the volume was compiled in Antwerp in the late 1640s, around twenty years after Ana's death. It was sent at an unknown date to Spain. On the page opposite each painting is a four-line poem. The last poem bears a signature: "G.H. Wilmart scripsit." Georges Herman Wilmart was an illuminator of manuscripts and a calligrapher who

worked in Brussels from 1623-87. Since the signature only affirms that he transcribed the text, it is uncertain whether he painted the miniatures as well.

[10] This work belongs to a series of thirty-five ink and wash drawings that bear explanatory inscriptions in Italian, Latin, and French. These formed the compositional basis for a series of prints of Ana's life, also in the archives of the Antwerp Carmel, which contain inscriptions in German and Latin.

[11] The paintings are now kept within the enclosure of the Disclaced Carmelite convent in Brussels.

[12] A Sister of Notre Dame de Namur, *Life of the Venerable Ana de Jesús,* 15.

[13] Ana de San Bartolomé, *Autobiografía A,* in OCASB, 1:285-86.

[14] A Sister of Notre Dame de Namur, *Life of the Venerable Ana de Jesús,* 19.

[15] *"Al espejo de Teresa/Se miro, y tomo consejo,/Su Imagen fue y no Bosquejo/Pues su virtud lo confiessa."*

[16] *"La Elias reformadora/En muestras de su desseo/A su hija como a Elisseo/De Espiritu la mejora."*

[17] Ange Manrique, *La vie de la Vénérable Mère Ana de Jésus, disciple et compagne de la Mère Sainte Thérèse de Jésus* (Brussels, 1639), 304, quoted in Marie-Ana de Jésus, 62.

[18] Quoted in translation in A Sister of Notre Dame de Namur, *Life of the Venerable Ana de Jesús,* 202.

[19] Ana de San Bartolomé, *Defensa de la herencia teresiana,* in OCASB, 1:415-16.

[20] Torres Sánchez, 37-9. In 1630 Beatriz de la Concepción returned to the Discalced Carmelite convent in Salamanca, making her the only one of the original nuns (who traveled from Spain to France with two Anas in 1604) to go back to Spain.

[21] Michel Florisoone, *Jean de la Croix: Iconographie Générale* (Bruges: Desclée de Brouwer, 1975), 268.

[22] The choice of subject has special significance since Ana died on the Feast of the Most Holy Trinity (7 June).

[23] Ana de San Bartolomé, *Autobiografía A* in OCASB, 1:307-8.

[24] Information about the series of Teresian engravings by Adriaen Collaert and Cornelis Galle series is contained in Emond,155. Ana de Jesús' involvement in the commission is mentioned in Laura Gutiérrez Rueda, "Iconografía de Santa Teresa," *Revista de Espiritualidad* 90 (1964): 5-168 (at p. 8), and in A Sister of Notre Dame de Namur, *Life of the Venerable Ana de Jesús,* 221. One of Ana de Jesús' letters, which must refer to this particular set of engravings, is quoted in *L'Art du XVII siècle dans les Carmels de France,* ed. Yves

Rocher, exh. cat. (Paris: Musée du Petit Palais, 1982), 47: "Je vous enverrai à la première occasion la vie de notre sainte Mère, représentée par plusieurs images avec ses révélations et miracles. Nous avons soin d'en faire exécuter un ouvrage complet."

25   Torres Sanchez, 11-12, 80-84. On the Discalced Carmelite expansion into France, see Barbara B. Diefendorf, *From Penitence to Charity: Pious Women and the Catholic Reformation in Paris* (New York: Oxford University Press, 2004), especially 102-118.

26   Cordula van Wyhe, "Court and Convent: The Infanta Isabella and Her Franciscan Confessor Andrés de Soto," *Sixteenth Century Journal* 35 (2004): 411-45, at 430. As further evidence of Isabella's particular admiration for Ana de Jesús, van Wyhe notes that in 1621 the Archduchess sent the flower that had decorated Ana's corpse to her sister-in-law, Margaret of the Cross, who had entered the convent of the Descalzas Reales in Madrid (436).

27   Ana de San Bartolomé, *Relaciones de gracias místicas,* in OCASB, 1:511.

28   *"Gusta Dios de Su Oración/Con [que?] le [haze?] mas logar/Queriendo a Amberes librar/En apretada ocasión."*

29   Cordula van Wyhe, *Jean Terrier, Portraicts des SS Vertus de la Vierge contemplées par feue S.A.S.M. Isabelle Clere Eugenie Infante d'Espagne* (Glasgow: Glasgow Emblem Studies, 2002).

30   van Wyhe, *Jean Terrier,* xxxiv-xxxvi.

31   Isabella Clara Eugenia's remark, recorded in a written declaration by Clara de la Cruz, is paraphrased in OCASB, 1:61*.

32   Marie of the Incarnation, *The Relation of 1654,* in *Marie of the Incarnation: Selected Writings,* ed. Irene Mahoney (New York: Paulist Press, 1989), 116-7.

1. Flemish, *The Christ Child accompanies the young Ana de San Bartolomé in the fields,* mid-seventeenth century. Madrid, Discalced Carmelite Convent.

Figure 2

2. Flemish, *The Christ Child accompanies the young Ana de San Bartolomé in the fields,* mid-seventeenth century. Antwerp, Discalced Carmelite Convent.

Figure 3

3. Flemish, *The Virgin's cure of the young Ana de Jesús,* mid-seventeenth century. Brussels, Discalced Carmelite Convent.

Figure 4

4. Flemish, *Ana de San Bartolomé rejects suitors in favor of Christ,* mid-seventeenth century. Antwerp, Discalced Carmelite Convent.

Figure 5

5. Flemish, *Ana de Jesús takes up the garb of a penitent,* mid-seventeenth century. Brussels, Discalced Carmelite Convent.

Figure 6

6. Flemish, *Ana de San Bartolomé, as the mirror image of St. Teresa of Ávila, receives the saint's blessing,* mid-seventeenth century. Madrid, Discalced Carmelite Convent.

7. Flemish, *Teresa (like another Elijah) blesses Ana de San Bartolomé (like another Elisha),* mid-seventeenth century. Madrid, Discalced Carmelite Convent.

Figure 8

8. Flemish, *Ana de Jesús receives the constitutions from St. Teresa of Ávila,* mid-seventeenth century. Brussels, Discalced Carmelite Convent.

Figure 9

9. P.I. Arenezen, *St. Teresa of Ávila with John of the Cross (identified as "Venerable") and Ana de Jesús,* nineteenth-century copy of a Flemish engraving by P. Roland van Overstraeten, created before 1675.

Figure 10

10. Jean Baptiste Barbé (1578-1649, Antwerp), *St. Teresa of Ávila and Ana de San Bartolomé in the presence of the Holy Trinity,* mid-seventeenth century.

Figure 11

11. Flemish, *Death of St. Teresa of Ávila (with Ana de San Bartolomé)*, mid-seventeenth century. Madrid, Discalced Carmelite Convent.

Figure 12

12. Flemish, *Death of St. Teresa of Ávila (with Ana de San Bartolomé),* mid-seventeenth century. Antwerp, Discalced Carmelite Convent.

Figure 13

13. Adriaen Collaert, *Death of St. Teresa of Ávila,* Antwerp, 1613.

Figure 14

14. Flemish, *Ana de Jesús with the shields of Spain, Flanders, and France,* mid-seventeenth century. Brussels, Discalced Carmelite Convent.

Figure 15

15. Flemish, *Ana de San Bartolomé defends Antwerp through prayer,* mid-seventeenth century. Madrid, Discalced Carmelite Convent.

Figure 16

16. Jean de Loisy, *The Virgin leads Isabella Clara Eugenia and squadrons of angelic virgins and nuns in battle against demons,* from Jean Terrier, *Portraicts des SS Vertus de la Vierge contemplées par feue S.A.S.M. Isabelle Clere Eugenie Infante d'Espagne,* Pin, 1635. Besançon, Bibliothèque Municipale.

Figure 17

17. Flemish, *Christ displays the Netherlands to Ana de San Bartolomé,* first half seventeenth century.

Touched by Teresa: Readers and Their Responses, 1588-1750[1]

Jodi Bilinkoff
University of North Carolina at Greensboro

Teresa of Ávila is well known, and beloved, as a reader of books. Recalling her girlhood love for novels of chivalry and the like she exclaimed: "I was so taken up with this reading that I didn't think I could be happy if I didn't have a new book."[2] How many readers have noted this famous passage from her *Life* and thrilled to think that they had something in common with a great saint! As a mature woman and monastic reformer Teresa would emphasize the importance of reading in the *Constitutions* she composed for her Discalced Carmelite nuns. She directed prioresses to "see to it that good books are available, especially *The Life of Christ* by the Carthusian [Ludolph of Saxony], the *Flos Sanctorum, The Imitation of Christ, The Oratory of Religious,* and those books written by Fray Luis de Granada and by Father Fray Pedro de Alcántara." "This sustenance for the soul," she insisted, "is in some way as necessary as is food for the body."[3]

In this essay, however, I turn from Teresa as reader to Teresa as author whose books were read by others. It is important to emphasize that Teresa's works, first published by Luis de León in 1588, enjoyed tremendous success not only in Spain, but throughout Catholic Europe and its colonies in the seventeenth and eighteenth centuries. Perhaps most popular was her *Life,* which was translated into many European languages. During the course of the seventeenth century Teresa's auto-biography saw at least eight editions in Italian and fourteen in French alone. It was, by early modern standards, a "best-seller."[4]

But, while sheer numbers are compelling, they do not tell the whole story. Who was actually reading the works of Teresa of Ávila? We can document at least two groups of readers. Teresa's books were read by other devout women, many of whom later became writers and recorded their own life narratives. They were also read by male clerics, the confessors and promoters of women they regarded as holy and held up as exemplars to a wider Christian community. Both spiritually-inclined women and their clerical supporters found inspiration in the life of Teresa of Ávila, and used her *Life* as a powerful authorizing precedent.

How did women readers first encounter Teresa and her texts? Many described growing up in families in which the reading of devotional literature was strongly encouraged. Teresa herself remembered a father who was "fond of reading good books" and thus "had books [in the vernacular] for his children to read."[5] For women in later generations Teresa's would be among the "good books" found in pious Catholic households.

Francisca Josepha de Castillo, brought up in New Granada (modern Colombia) during the second half of the seventeenth century, recalled: "My mother used to read to me the books of Saint Teresa of Jesus, and her *Foundations*, and this gave me a great desire to be like one of those nuns...."[6] As a child and young woman in Bavaria Anna Maria Lindmayr was profoundly moved by the writings of the Spanish mystics she read in German translation, including "das Leben der Heiligen Theresia."[7] The English recusant Catharine Burton read the lives of both Teresa of Ávila and Catherine of Siena by the time she was sixteen, and then began to imitate the ascetic practices and devotional regimes of these saintly models.[8] Margaret van der Noort worked as a domestic servant in Flanders. One of her employers, an aristocratic woman, had translated for her a biography of Teresa of Ávila, most likely Francisco de Ribera's immensely popular work, first published in

1590, rendering the text from Spanish to Margaret's native Dutch. Reading Teresa's life made such a strong impression upon the young woman that she resolved to enter the Discalced Carmelite convent in Brussels.[9] All four of these early readers of Teresa would, in fact, take religious vows: Anna Maria and Catharine (in religion, Mary Xaveria of the Angels), like Margaret, as nuns of Teresa's own Discalced Carmelite Order; Francisca Josepha as a Poor Clare. And all four would write their own spiritual autobiographies.

Other sorts of family connections and early life experiences brought women to Teresa and her writings as well. The future nun Teresa de Jesús María was born in the Castilian city of Toledo in 1592 and given the name María. As young as three years old, she would later claim, she heard the Lord call her to the religious life, specifically to be a nun in an ascetic order. Several influences would point her toward the recently-founded Discalced Carmelites. María often attended the church attached to their monastery. Her parents were apparently acquainted with certain Discalced Carmelite friars. And her mother made an astonishing admission to her sensitive and impressionable young daughter; that she too had once dreamed of the convent, and often felt distressed by her inability to fulfill this vocation. Her own convictions, her family's associations, and, one can imagine, the promptings of her pious mother led to María's entrance into Toledo's Discalced Carmelite convent at the unusually young age of nine. Teresa had, of course, spent much time in Toledo and had personally founded this house. Visible reminders of the saint filled the everyday landscape of the young *toledana*. Not surprisingly, María developed a particular affinity for this holy *compatriota*. She later recalled in her autobiography that at her profession eight years later, at the age of seventeen, "out of devotion for our Mother Saint Teresa [the sisters] gave me that name."[10]

After she lost her mother at the tender age of eight, the Catalan Teresa Mir began to frequent the Discalced Carmelite convent near her home in the town of Olot; her only sister would later take vows there. She would eventually follow the life of a pious beata, adopting the saint of Ávila, her namesake, as her special "patrona."[11] For Juana Rodríguez, recollections of Teresa, her family, and her earliest desires for a religious vocation were inextricably linked. When Teresa came to Burgos to establish a convent in the winter of 1582, she apparently met Juana's parents, well-to-do merchants of that city. According to the lovingly repeated story, on that occasion the nun embraced the eight-year old Juana, offered her blessing, and admonished her parents, "take care of that little girl, because God is going to work many miracles through her." Juana Rodríguez eventually entered a Dominican convent in Burgos, where she gained renown for her deep piety and, like the saint she had met as a child, composed an autobiography recounting her many mystical experiences.[12]

Women who entered the religious life often became acquainted with Teresa and her works in convents, where they had many opportunities both to read books and to hear them read aloud. Discalced Carmelites on both sides of the Atlantic participated in reading together the *Life* of their founder. Members of other religious orders, however, found themselves touched by Teresa as well. Ursula Suárez read Teresa's works in a Franciscan convent in Santiago, Chile. She bravely resolved to imitate the saint's virtues, declaring, "It seems from that day forward, I was to be like St. Teresa." She could not always meet these high standards, however.[13]

For another Spanish American nun reading Teresa made a deeper and longer-lasting impression. Mariana de la Encarnación was a Conceptionist in Mexico City in the early years of the seventeenth century. She later recalled how Teresa's *Life* started circulating in manuscript form (*cuadernos*) among the sisters, as the printed version was not yet available in New Spain. She described the extraordinary impact the text had on her own life:

> ...reading [these books] seemed so relevant to me, it seemed to me in my ignorance that my own path had some similarities with the beginning of her life. The tenderness, devotion and love that I conceived for this divine creature was so great that, reading these pages, I went one day before the Blessed Sacrament and...made a well-considered vow to Our Lord that if at some time a convent of that blessed order were to come I would work with all my strength and diligence to become a nun there, in imitation of our Holy Mother, and in order to persuade her to help me, I promised that every year I would celebrate the feast day of our patriarch the glorious Saint Joseph, whose devotion she had so promoted.

When the convent of San José opened in Mexico City in 1616, Mariana de la Encarnación, along with several other Conceptionists, fulfilled her vow and entered there as a Discalced Carmelite.[14]

In early modern Catholic Europe and its colonies male confessors or spiritual directors frequently maintained close relationships with pious women. In the course of these interactions they often recommended or even ordered their female penitents to read certain books, lending their own copies on occasion or bestowing them as gifts. In instances such as these the encounter with Teresa's writings represented a shared experience, an occasion for exchange between priest and penitent. André Duval, for example, remembered that as soon as Teresa's works and the biography by Ribera became available in French translation in 1601, the devout Parisian noblewoman Barbe

Acarie requested someone (probably Duval himself) to read her some sections of these books. "She listened attentively," he reported honestly, "but did not take great pleasure in them at first." Duval attributed his penitent's lukewarm response to the devil, but this was soon to change dramatically, as we shall see. Her initial reading did, however, leave Madame Acarie "astonished that the Holy Mother had been able to found so great an order in the Church."[15]

By the spring of 1604 François de Sales had also read these French translations of Teresa's works as well as the biography by Ribera, and he referred to them in letters of spiritual direction he wrote to his exceptional penitent Jeanne de Chantal. "I desire you to look at chapter 41 of *The Way of Perfection* of the blessed Saint Teresa," he counseled on one occasion, suggesting that this text would help Jeanne overcome her scruples and proceed with greater vigor and boldness to "the exercise of virtues."[16]

María Antonia Pereira, born in poverty in rural Galicia in 1700, was, like most people of her estate, illiterate. However, around the age of twenty-nine she conceived a great desire to read and begged God to instruct her. One day she opened a book, recognized the words "Love of God," and then read it all in a rush, realizing that "the Lord had conceded to her the favor of learning to read, with no other teacher than Himself."[17] María Antonia reported this and other supernatural graces to her confessor, José Ventura y Castro, an enthusiastic young man who had just received ordination. Castro struggled with how best to guide this wife and mother who claimed remarkable spiritual gifts. Just then someone gave him the *Life* of Teresa of Ávila. The priest saw this as providential, as he found so many helpful parallels between Teresa's experiences and those of his penitent. After he read the book, he gave it to María Antonia, who was also much consoled by it. She came to enjoy reading Teresa together with a small group of female followers (*discípulas*), anticipating, as it were, her later life as widow, nun (under the religious name María Antonia de Jesús), founder of the first Discalced Carmelite convent in Galicia, and author of her own autobiography and devotional writings.[18]

Most illiterate women, of course, required human aid to hear Teresa's words. The Portuguese friar Brás Soares read aloud her *Life* (as well as that of Catherine of Siena and other figures) to his fervent but unlettered penitent, the tertiary Isabel de Miranda.[19] Anne Jacobson Schutte speculates that the Venetian holy woman (and later inquisitorial defendant) Cecilia Ferrazzi absorbed Teresa's autobiography by similar means. Teresa clearly made a big impression on Ferrazzi in any case. She tried to found a Discalced Carmelite convent in Venice (a goal later accomplished by her younger sister), adopted Teresa's constitutions for the shelter she established for at-risk girls and women, and was accused of first commissioning a painter to make her portrait and then altering the face to resemble that of the Spanish saint![20]

And for some women, reading the books of Teresa of Ávila would lead to a direct encounter with the author, in the form of visions and other supernatural experiences. Recall that Barbe Acarie's initial impression of Teresa's *Life* was a rather tepid one. A few days later, however, "finding herself in prayer, the holy Mother Teresa visibly appeared to her, and announced to her that God wanted her to involve herself in founding convents of her order in France." Barbe and her spiritual advisors took some time to assess this vision, deciding whether it had been "intellectual" or "sensible" in nature, for example. But seven or eight months later "the holy Mother appeared to her for a second time, and commanded her even more strongly and insistently…and assured her that despite all the difficulties she would encounter, she would succeed [in this goal]." At that point the noblewoman threw herself into this project and worked tirelessly to bring the reform to her native country. After the death of her husband she entered the Discalced Carmelite house at Pontoise, adopting the name in religion Marie de l'Incarnation.[21]

To Isabel de Jesús (Sosa), a nun at the Discalced Carmelite house in Toledo, Teresa revealed herself by way of the text itself. As Isabel read she perceived the words of the saint illuminated by a ray of light emanating from a figure of Christ.[22] The Portuguese Poor Clare Antónia Margarida de Castelo Branco suffered from excessive fears and scruples, a condition much alleviated by reading Teresa's *Life*. Thereafter taking the saint as her spiritual guide (*mestra espiritual*), the nun insisted that "a number of times I have experienced her favor in many matters that could not be helped by natural means."[23] Across the Atlantic in Oaxaca, Mexico, a vision of a sympathetic Teresa who promised to keep watch over her notebooks gave much-needed assurance to the Augustinian Recollect María de San José and authorized her efforts to record her own life during the latter part of the seventeenth and early eighteenth centuries.[24] A few generations later her countrywoman María Coleta de San José also suffered doubts regarding her vocation as a writer. Even a vision of Christ in which he encouraged the Capuchin to record her inner experiences had not completely assuaged her anxieties. At last, she reported, "I felt that Santa Teresa had appeared before me with a compelling force…and I seemed to understand, or she told me, that just as clearly as she had told her confessors what had happened to her, that I should do the same."[25]

This issue of authorization also loomed large for male clerics, who used Teresa's life and works to guide and promote their own spiritual daughters. In 1641, for example, Francisco Ignacio became chaplain to a convent of Augustinian Recollects in the town of Arenas, in the mountains south of Ávila. As part of his duties he began to direct Isabel de Jesús, a lay sister of humble origins who claimed to receive extraordinary graces in prayer. The house's previous chaplain had had "a poor opinion of her spirit" and tried to persuade her that her many visions and raptures were either imaginary or sent by the devil. Fray Francisco, however, quickly became convinced of Isabel's piety and the authenticity of her experiences. He reassured his penitent by telling her that her "spirit [was] as good as that of the holy mother Teresa of Ávila."[26]

Confessor-hagiographers often placed their penitents within a genealogy of saintly women, in which, by the early seventeenth century, Teresa held a prominent place. Paul Ragueneau compared the visionary in New France, Catherine de Saint Augustin, to various medieval exemplars, and "in our times" (*en nos derniers siècles*) to Teresa of Ávila. Interestingly, the Jesuit was writing in 1671, nearly a hundred years after the death of the Spanish nun, yet she was still for him a vivid figure, a virtual contemporary.[27] The Mercedarian friar Juan Bautista del Santísimo Sacramento first served as amanuensis for the illiterate beata Mariana de Jesús as she dictated her life, and later added his own recollections. He was well aware that, by engaging in this collaboration, Mariana was joining a long line of holy women and autobiographers, while he himself was entering the ranks of famous confessors, biographers, and scribes. A prologue begins with these words:

> The whole history of the Blessed Angela of Foligno was known to her confessor, he having heard it from her own mouth, in the same way as did Father Raymond of Capua, who was the confessor of the Blessed Catherine of Siena, and also this is how was written the life and miracles and revelations of the Blessed Mother Teresa de Jesús...and the same could be said about many other lives and revelations....

Juan Bautista's words indicate a distinct pride of pedigree, and suggest that the friar welcomed validation for himself, as well as for his exemplary penitent.[28]

Clerical authors used comparisons with Teresa to certify entire nations as holy, not just individuals. Failure to publicize the life of Barbe Acarie, André Duval insisted, would "deprive France of a very great honor and debase it, placing it below the other nations that have in our time been favored by Heaven by such illustrious saints" as Italy's Charles Borromeo and Spain's Ignatius Loyola and, of course, Teresa of Ávila.[29] In 1677 Claude Martin published the autobiography of the mystic and missionary to New France Marie de l'Incarnation (who was also his biological mother), along with his own commentaries and conclusion. In this fascinating hybrid text he likened the French Ursuline to Teresa no fewer than three times. In a preface Martin claimed that Marie wrote about the mystical life in "a manner so clear and intelligible…that one could easily call her a second Saint Teresa." He repeated, but also subtly expanded, this sentiment at the end of the book, now referring to Marie as "a second Saint Teresa, or rather, the Teresa of Canada," and "the Saint Teresa of the New World." In Martin's formulation, Canadian soil had been sacralized by the present of a saint, and a saint whose holy life and mystical graces invited comparison with the great Teresa. With credentials such as these, this new land could truly become integrated into an emerging trans-Atlantic Catholic community.[30]

In early modern Catholic Europe and its colonies, then, women and men eagerly read the works of Teresa of Ávila, responding to and utilizing them in myriad ways. Her writings offered guidance, consolation, and strategies for coping with personal problems. Reading Teresa helped many women decide whether or not to take monastic vows, and taught them how to put into words deeply felt spiritual longings and experiences. Most of all, the books of Teresa of Ávila authorized other pious women to write, and especially, to write their own lives. Fray Luis de León proclaimed that the saint had left behind "two living images of herself," namely, "her daughters and her books."[31] One might add, daughters who read her books, and who wrote their own.

For male clerics, Teresa's writings provided helpful tips on how to understand and advise their exceptional female penitents. And they used the saint as an unshakable precedent, a figure whose life, and *Life*, legitimated the aspirations of their own spiritual daughters, and, incidentally, highlighted their own skills of discernment and direction.

As a child Teresa de Ahumada had loved to read books. During the course of her life she underwent a profound transformation, from reader of popular novels, to reader of devotional literature and saints' lives, to writer of devotional literature and her own *Life*. Eventually her works would touch countless lives, providing "sustenance for the soul" for generations to come.

---

[1]   I discuss much of this material, in somewhat different context, in my book *Related Lives: Confessors and Their Female Penitents, 1450-1750* (Ithaca: Cornell University Press, 2005).

[2]   Teresa of Ávila, *Life,* 2.1; unless otherwise indicated, all English translations from Teresa's writings are taken from *The Collected Works of St. Teresa of Ávila,* trans. Kieran Kavanaugh, O.C.D., and Otilio Rodríguez, O.C.D. (Washington, DC: Institute of Carmelite Studies, 1976). Santa Teresa de Jesús, *Obras completas,* ed. Efrén de la Madre de Dios and Otger Steggink (Madrid: Editorial Católica, 1977), 30, "Era tan estremo lo que en esto me embevía, que, si no tenía libro nuevo, no me parece tenía contento." For an analysis of Teresa's early reading practices and their influence on her later works see Carole A. Slade, "'Este Gran Dios de la Cavallerías' [This Great God of Chivalric Deeds]: St. Teresa's Performances of the Novels of Chivalry," in *The Vernacular Spirit: Essays on Medieval Religious Literature,*

ed. Renate Blumenfeld-Kosinski, Duncan Robertson, and Nancy Bradley Warren (New York: Palgrave, 2002), 297-316.

3   Teresa of Ávila, *Constitutions,* 8, and *Obras completas,* 636, "Tenga cuenta la priora con que haya buenos libros, en especial *Cartujanos, Flos Santorum, Contentus Mundi, Oratorio de Religiosos,* los de fray Luis de Granada y del padre fray Pedro de Alcántara, porque es en parte tan necesario este mantenimiento para el alma como el comer para el cuerpo."

4   "Repertorio dei testi a stampa," in *Donna, disciplina, creanza cristiana dal XV a XVII secolo: Studi e testi a stampa,* ed. Gabriella Zarri (Rome: Edizioni di Storia e Letteratura, 1996), 2434-2449; Henri-Jean Martin, *Livre, pouvoirs et société à Paris au XVIIe siècle* (Geneva: Droz, 1999), 1:20, 158. See *Related Lives,* ch. 5 for a broader discussion of the publication, translation, and distribution of exemplary life narratives in early modern Catholic Europe and its colonies.

5   Teresa of Ávila, *Life* 1.1, and *Obras completas,* 28-29, "Era mi padre aficionado a leer buenos libros, y ansí los tenía de romance para que leyesen sus hijos éstos."

6   *Obras completas de la Madre Francisca Josepha de la Concepción de Castillo,* ed. Dario Achury Valenzuela (Bogotá: Banco de la República, 1968; orig. completed ca.1715), 1:5, "Leía mi madre los libros de santa Teresa de Jesús, y sus *Fundaciones,* y a mí me daba un tan grande deseo de ser como una de aquellas monjas...." See also Kathryn Joy McKnight, *The Mystic of Tunja: The Writings of Madre Castillo* (Amherst: University of Massachusetts Press, 1997).

7   Cited in Charlotte Woodford, *Nuns as Historians in Early Modern Germany* (Oxford: Oxford University Press, 2002), 28.

8   Claire Walker, *Gender and Politics in Early Modern Europe: English Convents in France and the Low Countries* (Houndmills, UK: Palgrave Macmillan, 2003), 152.

9   My thanks to Cordula van Wyhe for providing me with this anecdote. For more on the introduction of the Discalced Carmelites in the Spanish Netherlands see her article "Court and Convent: The Infanta Isabella and Her Franciscan Confessor Andrés de Soto," *Sixteenth Century Journal* 35-2 (2004): 411-445, esp. 429-434.

10   *Las obras de...Sor Teresa de Jesús María [1592-c.1642],* ed. Manuel Serrano y Sanz (Madrid: Gil Blas, 1921), 3-9, "Cuando yo entré monja me llamaba María...y después, por devoción de nuestra Madre Santa Teresa, me pusieron

este nombre cuando profesé…." After her mother was widowed she too became a Discalced Carmelite nun, but entered a different convent. One of her two brothers became a Discalced Carmelite friar; the other, a Jesuit priest.

[11] James S. Amelang, "Los usos de la autobiografía: monjas y beatas en la Cataluña moderna," in *Historia y género: Las mujeres en la Europa moderna y contemporánea,* ed. James S. Amelang and Mary Nash (Valencia: Edicions Alfons el Magnànim, 1990), 197-198.

[12] Isabelle Poutrin, "Juana Rodríguez, una autora mística olvidada (Burgos, siglo XVII)," in *Estudios sobre escritoras hispánicas en honor de Georgina Sabat-Rivers,* ed. Lou Charnon-Deutsch (Madrid: Castalia, 1992), 269-270. Juana's convent sisters recalled "Si saben, o han oído decir, que en la niñez…dio Nuestro Señor maravillosas señales de su futura santidad…que santa Teresa de Jesús (que estaba a la sazón en esta ciudad a la fundación del convento des sus Monjas), tomándole en brazos, y bendiciéndola, dijo a sus Padres tuviesen mucho cuidado con aquella niña, porque Dios había de obrar muchas maravillas en ella."

[13] Ursula Suárez, *Relación autobiográfica,* ed. Mario Ferreccio Podestá (Santiago de Chile: Universidad de Concepción, 1984; orig.completed ca.1730), 165, "Mas, cuando llegaba el tiempo de confesarme…esclamaba a Dios de lo íntimo de mi corazón, pidiéndole perdón con tal propósito…que paresia que desde aquel día había de ser una santa Teresa." See also Kristine Ibsen, *Women's Spiritual Autobiography in Colonial Spanish America* (Gainesville: University Press of Florida, 1999), ch. 6; Kathleen Ann Myers, *Neither Saints Nor Sinners: Writing the Lives of Women in Spanish America* (New York: Oxford University Press, 2003), ch.5.

[14] Mariana de la Encarnación's chronicle, "Historia del convento [de San José] de las carmelitas descalzas de la ciudad de México desde su fundación," is transcribed in Manuel Ramos Medina, *Místicas y descalzas: Fundaciones femeninas carmelitas en la Nueva España* (Mexico City: CONDUMEX, 1997), 331-369; 330, "leyendo en ellos [libros] hicieron tan a mi propósito, que me parecía con mi ignorancia tenía alguna semejanza mi camino, que era de los principios de su vida.   Fue tan grande la ternura, devoción y amor que cobré con esta divina criatura que, leyendo sus papeles, me fui un día delante del Santísimo Sacramento y…hice voto (muy bien pensado) a nuestro Señor que en cualquier tiempo que hubiese convento de esta sagrada religión procurar con todas mis fuerzas y diligencias ser religiosa en ella y, a imitación de nuestra Santa Madre por obligarla a que me ayudase, prometí de celebrar

todos los años la fiesta de nuestro patriarca el glorioso san José (cuya devoción ella tanto encarga)."

[15] André Duval, *La vie admirable de la Bienheureuse Soeur Marie de l'Incarnation...appelée dans le monde Mademoiselle Acarie* (Paris: Librairie Victor Lecoffre, 1893; orig.1621), 120-121, "Les livres de la sainte mère Thérèse, avec sa vie composée par le Père Ribera, de la Compagnie de Jésus, ayant été traduits d'espagnol en français...se vendirent à Paris et furent lus par les personnes de dévotion...la Bienheureuse désira qu'on lui en lût quelques chapitres...[e]lle les écouta attentivement, mais elle n'y prenait pas grand goût au commencement, et s'étonnait comment celle sainte Mère avait pu fonder un si grand Ordre en l'Eglise. C'était sans doute le diable qui...lui causait ces dégoûts et ces refroidissements...."

[16] François de Sales, *Correspondance: Les lettres d'amitié spirituelle,* ed. André Ravier (Paris: Desclée de Brouwer, 1980), 180-81, "Je desire que vous voyez le chapitre 41 du *Chemin de Perfection* de la bienhereuse sainte Thérèse; car il vous aidera à bien entendre le mot que je vous ai dit si souvent, qu'il y faut point trop pointiller en l'experience des vertus, mais qu'il y faut aller rondement, franchement, naivement, à la vieille française, avec liberté, à la bonne foi, grosso modo." This letter of 1 November 1604 is available in English translation in Francis de Sales, Jane de Chantal, *Letters of Spiritual Direction,* trans. Péronne Marie Thibert (New York: Paulist Press, 1988), 126. For more on this relationship see Wendy Wright, *Bond of Perfection: Jeanne de Chantal and François de Sales* (New York: Paulist Press, 1985).

[17] Una Carmelita Descalza del Convento de Santiago, *Una mística gallega en el siglo XVIII: La Venerable Madre María Antonia de Jesús* (La Coruña: Fundación "Pedro Barrié de la Maza, Conde de Fenosa," 1991), 53, quoting from local beatification hearings initiated soon after her death in 1760: "Tomando un librito lo abrió por las primeras hojas y leyó 'Amor de Dios' y así fue leyendo en él de corrido, entiendo perfectamente el sentido de lo que leía...el Señor le había concedido el favor de aprender de leer, sin otro maestro que El...."

[18] Una Carmelita Descalza del Convento de Santiago, *Una mística gallega,* 67.

[19] Maria de Lurdes Correia Fernandes, "A construção da santidade nos finais do século XVI: O caso de Isabel de Miranda, tercedeira, viúva e 'santa' (ca.1539-1610)," in *Actas do Colóquio Internacional Piedade Popular: Sociabiladades, representações, espiritualidades* (Lisbon: Centro de História da Cultura/Terramar, 1999), 248, 257-258.

[20] Anne Jacobson Schutte, "Inquisition and Female Autobiography: The Case of Cecilia Ferrazzi," in *The Crannied Wall: Women, Religion, and the Arts in Early Modern Europe,* ed. Craig A. Monson (Ann Arbor: University of Michigan Press, 1992), 107,109.

[21] Duval, 120-122, "A quelques jours de là, comme elle se trouvait en oraison, voici la sainte mère Thérèse qui lui apparait visiblement, et l'avertit que Dieu voulait qu'elle s'employât à fonder en France des monastères de son Ordre. Dire la qualitè de cette vision, si elle fut intellectuelle ou sensible, nous ne le pouvons pas…Mais voici que sept ou huit mois après, la sainte Mère lui apparut pour la seconde fois, lui commandant plus fortement et puissament qu'à la première de mettre derechef cette affaire en délibération, et l' assurant que nonobstant toutes les difficultés qu'on trouvait, elle réussirait." For more on Acarie and Duval and their efforts to bring the Discalced Carmelites to France see Barbara B. Diefendorf, *From Penitence to Charity: Pious Women and the Catholic Reformation in Paris* (New York: Oxford University Press, 2004), ch.3.

[22] Sherry M. Velasco, *Demons, Nausea, and Resistance in the Autobiography of Isabel de Jesús (1611-1682)* (Albuquerque: University of New Mexico Press, 1996), 70-71.

[23] Antónia Margarida de Castelo Branco, *Autobiografia, 1652-1717,* ed. João Palma-Ferreira (Lisbon: Imprensa Nacional, 1983), 187, "…tomei esta Santa por mestra espiritual e várias vezes tenho experimentado o seu favor em muitas coisas que se não remediaram por via natural."

[24] Myers, 79-80.

[25] Ibsen, 14-15, 146, n. 49, "Sentí que con una violencia se me ponía delante Santa Teresa…y parece que entendía o me decía tan claro como decía sus cosas que le pasaban a los confesores que así lo había yo de hacer."

[26] *Vida de la Venerable Madre Isabel de Iesús…Dictada por ella misma y Añadido lo que falto…El P. Fr. Francisco Ignacio* (Madrid, 1675), 174,196, "Tu espiritu sea tan bueno como el de la Santa Madre Teresa de Iesus…"

[27] Paul Ragueneau, *La Vie de la Mère Catherine de Saint Augustin, Religieuse Hospitalière de la Miséricorde de Québec en la Nouvelle-France* (Paris, 1671),11.

[28] This hybrid text is transcribed in Elías Gómez Domínguez, *Beata Mariana de Jesús, Mercedaria Madrileña* (Rome: Instituto Histórico de la Orden de la Merced, 1991), 86-141; 87-88, "Toda la historia de la bienaventurada Angela de Foligno, la supo su Confesor, habiéndole oído de su propia boca; a la man-

era que el Padre Fray Raimundo de Capua, Confesor que fue de la bienaventurada Santa Catalina de Siena, y también, como se escribe la vida y milagros
y revelaciones de la Beata Madre Teresa de Jesús...y lo mismo se puede
referir de otras muchas vidas y revelaciones...."

29   Duval, xxii, "...et priveroit-on la France d'un tres grand honneur, et la
ravaleroit-on par ce moyen au dessous des autres nations, qui ont esté en ce
siecle favorisées du Ciel des Saincts fort ilustres; comme l'Italie de sainct
Charles Borromée, et l'Espagne du bien-heureux Ignace, fondateur de l'Ordre
de la Compagnie de Jesus, et la bien-heureuse mere Terese."

30   *La Vie de la Venerable Mere Marie de l'Incarnation...* (Paris, 1677; facsimi-
le edition, Solesmes, 1981), preface, n.p., "Et quand elle traite de la vie mystique c'est d'une maniere si claire & si intelligible...on la peut bien appeller
une seconde sainte Terese...;" 748, "qu'elle peut estre appellée une seconde
sainte Therese, ou plútost la Therese du Canada;" 753, "qui disoit que nôtre
Mere est une seconde sainte Therese, & qu'on la peut appeller la sainte
Therese du nouveau Monde." For more on this theme see *Colonial Saints:
Discovering the Holy in the Americas, 1500-1800,* ed. Allan Greer and Jodi
Bilinkoff (New York: Routledge, 2003).

31   Fray Luis de León, *Obras completas castellanas,* ed. Félix García (Madrid:
Editorial Católica, 1977), 1:904, "Yo no conocí ni vi a la Madre Teresa de
Jesús mientras estuvo en la tierra; mas agora que vive en el cielo la conozco
y veo casi siempre en dos imágines vivas que nos dejó de sí, que son sus hijas
y sus libros..."

St. Joseph in the Spirituality of Ávila and of Francis de Sales: Convergences and Divergences

Joseph F. Chorpenning, O.S.F.S.

Saint Joseph's University Press
International Commission on Salesian Studies

In offering to the French king, Louis XIII, his new translation of the writings of St. Teresa of Ávila (1515-82) published in 1630, Father Élisée de Saint Bernard reminds the monarch of the special bond that exists between Teresa and France: "Your Majesty will read . . . in these works that [the saint] founded her order to help France, which was at the time a theatre where heresy acted out bloody tragedies."[1] Indeed, this idea was commonplace among those promoting the renewal of Catholicism in early modern France, and is substantiated by the "mission statement" for the reformed Carmel that Teresa provides in her *Way of Perfection* (1566?). In the book's initial chapter, Teresa instructs her Carmelite daughters that the life of prayer and strict observance that they follow at the first reformed monastery of St. Joseph's in Ávila is an antidote for the attacks on the Church being waged in France. Teresa explains it in this way:

> When I began to take the first steps toward founding this monastery. . . . news reached me of the harm being done in France and of the havoc the Lutherans had caused and how much this miserable sect was growing. The news distressed me greatly, and, as though I could do something or were something, I cried to the Lord and begged Him that I might remedy so much evil. . . . As a result I resolved to do the little that was in my power; that is, to follow the evangelical counsels as perfectly as

I could and strive that these few persons who live here do the same. . . . Since we would all be occupied in prayer for those who are the defenders of the Church and for preachers and for learned men who protect her from attack, we could help as much as possible this Lord of mine. . . (1.2). [2]

The confusion of Lutherans and Calvinists or Huguenots aside, the avowed purpose of the Teresian Carmel made its introduction to France a priority for the Parisian group of committed laity and clergy that was instrumental in renewing Catholicism in this country devastated by the wars of religion.[3] In a real sense, then, there were innumerable heirs of St. Teresa in France and the French-speaking world. One of these would become equal in stature to Teresa: Francis de Sales (1567-1622), "the most respected francophone bishop of his time"[4] and the only French-speaking saint canonized in the seventeenth century.[5] Like Teresa, Francis was canonized a saint within a few decades of his death (1665), has been declared a doctor of the Church (1877), and sets forth a spirituality based on lived experience and characterized by common sense, a sense of humor, and a capacity to look on the bright side of things.[6]

Francis's Encounter with Teresa

Francis de Sales and Teresa were contemporaries. Although their lives overlapped for a period of fifteen years, Francis was probably not much aware of Teresa until well after her death. A French-speaking native of the duchy of Savoy, Francis saw his homeland deeply affected by Calvinism, which had attracted many laypeople who longed for an inner piety rarely found outside the cloister in Catholic lands. Educated at the best humanistic schools of the day— in Paris at the Jesuit Collège de Clermont, and at the University of

Padua, where he received a double doctorate in civil and canon law and also studied theology—Francis was ordained a priest in 1593. After a perilous but successful mission to reconvert the Calvinist Chablais region back to Catholicism, he was appointed coadjutor to the bishop of Geneva, who lived in exile in Annecy because of the Calvinist occupation of his see city.

In 1602 Francis traveled to Paris on ecclesiastical and state business, and it was there, in the home of Barbe Acarie, that he became part of the group of ecclesiastics and laypeople that was instrumental in bringing the Teresian Carmel to France. In fact, Francis was delegated by the group to seek permission for the new foundation from Pope Clement VIII.[7]

It is also worth mentioning that the year 2004 marked both the fourth centenary of the introduction of the Teresian Carmel to France and to New Spain (Puebla, Mexico), and of the first meeting of Francis and St. Jane Frances de Chantal (1572-1641), with whom he later founded the Order of the Visitation of Holy Mary (1610). The initial encounter of Francis and Jane took place in Dijon, where the young bishop had been invited to preach the course of sermons for the Lenten season of 1604. One of several reasons why Francis accepted this invitation was his intense interest in the proposal for a Carmelite foundation in the Burgundian capital.[8]

The monastery of St. Joseph was founded in Dijon in September of the following year, 1605, by Madre Ana de Jesús (1545-1621), one of Teresa's favorite daughters for whom St. John of the Cross (1542-91) had composed his *Spiritual Canticle*. Madame de Chantal—this is how, as a lady of baronial rank, Jane continued to be known even after she entered religion—enthusiastically supported and frequently visited the Dijon Carmel. And later as the mother foundress of the Visitation who traveled throughout France to make new foundations,

she was considered the "Mother Teresa" of her own country.[9] Thus the
early history of the Teresian and Salesian spiritual traditions is inter-
twined.

How did Francis come to know Teresa? First of all, he came
into immediate and living contact with her and her reform in the
Teresian Carmel that, as has been noted, he played a pivotal role in
establishing in France. Secondly, he encountered the "authentic
voice" of *La Madre* in her writings, specifically the trilogy of the *Book
of Her Life* (begun in 1562 and completed in 1565), *Way of Perfection*,
and *Interior Castle* (1577) that became available in French translation
in 1601. Also important was his reading of Francisco de Ribera's biography of Teresa that was published in French in 1602.[10]

Francis's reading of Teresa confirmed and enriched his spirituality that was steadily developing in a mystical direction, as well as his
approach to spiritual direction, particularly of women, for which he
was renowned for having a special gift. Francis often recommends
Teresa's writings to his readers and correspondents. In his master-
work *Treatise on the Love of God* (1616), he exalted Teresa as an
author and a martyr of divine love (Preface; Bk. 6, chs. 12, 14-15, and
Bk. 7, ch. 11). Elisabeth Stopp has aptly described the rapport that
exists between these two saints:

> In their own age and ever after, both have enjoyed immense
> popularity as real living people, as friends, in their writings;
> every reader has the impression we know them personally, as
> indeed we do. "Notre chère Mère Thérèse" [our dear Mother
> Teresa], as Francis called her, was a real and beloved friend to
> him, to his correspondents and to every Visitandine when he
> wrote and spoke about her.[11]

Veneration of St. Joseph by Teresa and Francis

An element that is common to both Teresian and Salesian spirituality is the privileged place that each gives to the person of St. Joseph. The role of Teresa and Francis in disseminating veneration of the saint in the early modern period is often memorialized in devotional literature and art. A notable example of this in North America is to be found in the crypt church of St. Joseph's Oratory in Montreal, the largest shrine in the world dedicated to the saint. In the sanctuary over the main altar, A. Giacomini's splendid Carrara marble statue of St. Joseph holding the Christ Child is flanked by statues of Teresa and Francis.[12]

Teresa's testimony to her ardent affection for St. Joseph is to be found in her *Life*, chapters 6, 32, and 33. The special veneration that Teresa accorded St. Joseph is also chronicled in Ribera's biography and, perhaps more importantly and influentially, in the *Josephina* or *Summary of the Excellencies of St. Joseph* by the Discalced Carmelite friar Jerónimo Gracián de la Madre de Dios (1545-1614) that was first published in Spanish and Italian in 1597 and in French translation in 1619. Francis would have certainly been well versed in *La Madre's* intense devotion to St. Joseph. He is even reported to have said that "he had a special devotion to St. Teresa because it was she who has renewed in our age devotion to this saint."[13] Pierre Sérouet comments that this remark suggests that St. Joseph led Francis to Teresa, rather than that Teresa led Francis to St. Joseph,[14] although again, here as elsewhere, Teresa would have confirmed and enriched Francis's own intuitions.

There are aspects of Francis's devotion to St. Joseph that he clearly shares with Teresa, e.g., his practice of referring to the saint as "the glorious St. Joseph," his naming St. Joseph as the titular patron of the church of the first monastery of the Visitation Order in Annecy, and his imbuing a fervent devotion to St. Joseph in his Visitation sisters. However, close comparison of the texts of Teresa and of Francis on St. Joseph reveals complementarity more than influence. The remainder of this paper will briefly reflect—*grosso modo*, as Francis liked to say when he was short of time—on three complementary points between Teresa and Francis: (1) the lengthy period of gestation that preceded the formal articulation of their appreciation of the person and mission of St. Joseph; (2) their particular emphases in these statements; and (3) the primary role that St. Joseph has in Teresian and Salesian spirituality.

A Theology Developed over a Prolonged Period of Time

The starting-point for Teresa's discussion, in the *Life*, chapter 6, of her devotedness to St. Joseph is her healing from paralysis through the saint's intercessory power. Shortly after entering the Carmelite monastery of the Incarnation in Ávila, Teresa was afflicted with a crippling illness for nearly three years, from about the middle of 1539 until approximately April 1542. At the time of her miraculous recovery, then, Teresa was twenty-seven years old. She would not commence writing her *Life* for another twenty years, which provided her ample opportunity to reflect on and solidify what she would eventually write about this episode that on the surface may seem to be the catalyst for her devotion to St. Joseph.

This healing, however, was not necessarily Teresa's first encounter with St. Joseph. Scholars who have studied this question suggest that well before this event Teresa may have encountered St. Joseph in several "places." To mention the principal ones identified in the scholarly literature: First, there is her home, where veneration of St. Joseph may well have been one of the devotions that Teresa was taught by her mother (*Life*, 1.6). Then, there is Teresa's spiritual reading. Her earliest reading included the lives of the saints (*Life*, 1.4), and it has recently been argued that the particular edition of the *Flos Sanctorum* that Teresa read included a newly added life of St. Joseph that reflected on his mission in salvation history and enumerated his privileges.[15] Of course, after her healing but before writing her *Life*, she read Bernardino de Laredo's *Ascent of Mt. Sion* (first edition, 1535; second edition, 1538; subsequent editions, 1540, 1542, 1590, 1617), to which was appended a *Josephina*, or brief treatise on *The Mysteries of St. Joseph*, that would have nurtured and enriched Teresa's devotion to and doctrine on the saint.[16]

Yet another place of encounter was the liturgy. The Franciscan pope Sixtus IV introduced the feast of St. Joseph (19 March) to Rome in 1479. Following this initiative, distinguished Spanish ecclesiastics of the reign of the Catholic Kings, such as Hernando de Talavera (1428-1507) and Francisco Jiménez de Cisneros (1436-1517), took steps to see that this feast was celebrated throughout Spain.[17] The feast of St. Joseph was also celebrated in the ancient Order of Carmel—often with a proper Mass and office. In the introit or entrance antiphon of one such Mass, St. Joseph is hailed as the "father of the Church" (*pater Ecclesiae*). The lessons for Matins in a Carmelite breviary published in Brussels in 1480 are taken from the treatise *The Twelve Privileges of St. Joseph* by the French cardinal Pierre d'Ailly (1350-1420), bishop of Cambrai, who, like Jean Gerson (1363-1429), the eloquent and prolific chancellor of the University of Paris, and St. Bernardine of Siena (1380-1444), the Franciscan preacher and doctor of the Church, was a vigorous promoter of devotion to St. Joseph in the late Middle Ages.[18]

These factors highlight that the privileged place that St. Joseph had in Teresa's life and Carmelite reform unfolded over many, many years, possibly beginning in childhood. Undoubtedly this lengthy period of gestation and assimilation accounts for the clarity, sureness, and maturity of what Teresa writes about the saint in her *Life*. It also helps us to understand better the remark attributed to Francis that Teresa "renewed" devotion to St. Joseph, as she disseminated it on a scale hoped for but not seen by her late medieval forebears.

A lengthy process of development and appropriation also preceded Francis's setting forth a rich and fully developed theology of St. Joseph during the final decade of his life (1612-22). Francis's references to the saint prior to this period are by no means insignificant, but they pale in comparison to the robust theology of St. Joseph proffered in the *Treatise on the Love of God* and in his sermons, culminating with that of 19 March 1622, on the virtues of St. Joseph. In the introductory study and commentary accompanying my translation of Francis's sermon texts on St. Joseph, I tried to document how they open a window onto Francis's thought process, methods of composition, preaching style, and theological development.[19] Here I want to underscore that, like Teresa, Francis's affection for and ideas about St. Joseph were years in the making.

It is likely that Francis first encountered St. Joseph in some of the same places that Teresa did, such as the liturgy, since the feast of St. Joseph had been celebrated in Francis's native diocese of Geneva since 1440. Another place was the churches of Annecy. The church of Saint-Maurice had a chapel dedicated to St. Joseph that dated to 1581, and the church of Notre-Dame had a chapel to the saint from 1586.[20] (As already mentioned, as bishop of Geneva, Francis built the church of St. Joseph in Annecy that was attached to the first monastery of the Visitation Order, blessing its cornerstone in 1614 and solemnly consecrating it in 1618.[21])

Another "place" where Francis met St. Joseph was in St. Ignatius Loyola's *Spiritual Exercises*, which he made annually throughout his life.[22] In the meditations on the infancy and hidden life of Christ that precede the great meditation on the Two Standards during the second week,[23] Francis would have constantly been in the company of St. Joseph.

Similar to Teresa's experience, Francis's spiritual reading would have also nurtured his relationship with and insights into St. Joseph. Besides learning of Teresa's devotion in her writings and Ribera's biography, Francis would have known the prolific writings on St. Joseph by Gerson, for whom the bishop had great esteem and admiration.[24] It is often proposed that the brief but memorable encomium of the saint in Lorenzo Scupoli's *Spiritual Combat* (1589, with numerous editions thereafter), which Francis calls "my well loved book" that he carried on his person and read daily,[25] had a formative influence on his veneration of St. Joseph.[26] As attractive as this idea is, it is not corroborated by the history of the editions of the *Spiritual Combat*. The copy that Francis possessed was the *editio princeps* of 1589, which had only 33 chapters; chapter 50, which has the relevant passage on St. Joseph, was not added until the 1599 edition.[27]

Two Appreciations of St. Joseph

In the *Life*, chapter 6, and in the works of Ribera and Gracián, the various roles that St. Joseph fulfilled in Teresa's life and experience are enumerated: the heavenly physician who healed her from paralysis; spiritual father (an unprecedented advocation for the saint in Christian history[28]) who "came to [her] rescue in better ways than [she] knew how to ask for" (*Life*, 6.6); an all-powerful intercessor who "helps in all our needs" (*Life*, 6.6); a celestial benefactor who repays souls who recommend themselves to him with advancement in virtue; a teacher of prayer who assisted Teresa in her longtime struggle with prayer; a protector on her many journeys. Filled with "the desire to

persuade all to be devoted to [St. Joseph]" (*Life*, 6.8), Teresa extended her privileged relationship with St. Joseph to the Teresian Carmel
by making him, in accord with a vision she received from the Lord
(*Life*, 32.11), the guardian of her foundations, thus underscoring St.
Joseph's role as father not only in her life, but also, henceforth, in the
life of the Teresian Carmel.

The one role that encompasses all St. Joseph's other roles is that
he is the most powerful intercessor who helps in every need, whether
spiritual or temporal, making him a universal saint. The theological
foundation for this extraordinary unfailing intercessory power is St.
Joseph's singular relationship to Jesus. Teresa writes:

> For with other saints it seems the Lord has given them grace to
> be of help in one need, whereas with this glorious saint I have
> experience that he helps in all our needs and that the Lord wants
> us to understand that just as He was subject to St. Joseph on
> earth—for since bearing the title of father, being the Lord's
> tutor, Joseph could give the Child command—so in heaven God
> does whatever he commands (*Life*, 6.6).

From this passage, it might even be inferred that Christ Himself is the
first propagator of devotion to St. Joseph. The theme of the saint's all-
powerful heavenly intercession is not new, having been advanced by
Teresa's late medieval predecessors Gerson and Bernardine of Siena.[29]
However, Teresa's articulation of this theme is so clear and forceful
that it will gain singular authority, leading to her characterization in
subsequent devotional literature as the one who founded or renewed
devotion to St. Joseph.[30]

The theme of St. Joseph's omnipotent intercessory power is also
in the forefront of Francis's theology of the saint, epitomized by his

sermon on "The Virtues of St. Joseph" of 1622—one of the most famous ever preached on the saint. Preaching in the church of St. Joseph in Annecy, where both his Visitation sisters, within the cloister choir, and the laity, in the body of the church, worshipped, Francis solemnly proclaims:

> What more remains for us to say now, except that we cannot doubt at all that this glorious saint has great influence in heaven. . . . Oh, how happy shall we be, if we can merit a share in his holy intercession!, for nothing will be refused him, either by Our Lady, or by her glorious Son. He will obtain for us, if we have confidence in him, a holy growth in all kinds of virtues, but especially in those that we have found that he possessed in a higher degree than any others, which are most holy purity of body and mind, the most lovable virtue of humility, constancy, courage, and perseverance: virtues which will make us victorious in this life over our enemies, and which will make us merit the grace to go and enjoy in eternal life the rewards prepared for those who shall imitate the example given them by St. Joseph while he was in this life, a reward that will be nothing less than eternal happiness, in which we shall enjoy the luminous vision of the Father, of the Son, and of the Holy Spirit.[31]

The similarity and the difference with Teresa are striking. For both Teresa and Francis, St. Joseph's intercessory power is unfailing. But here, as elsewhere in Francis's writings, the emphasis is *always* on the example provided by the saint's specific virtues and on growth in these virtues by the imitation of his example and by appealing to his heavenly intercession for this purpose. Let me try to express this in another way. The theme of learning from and imitating St. Joseph's

example is one of several hallmarks of Teresa's doctrine of the saint—
she specifically emphasizes his humble service of and prayerful intimacy with Jesus and Mary (*Life*, 6.8)—especially with respect to her
Carmelite reform. In Francis, this theme is more fully, even exhaus-
tively, developed by his constant focus on and appeal to St. Joseph's
virtues so that it becomes the leitmotiv of his doctrine of the saint.

St. Joseph in Teresian and Salesian Spirituality

As a result of her deep personal relationship over so many years
with St. Joseph, Teresa found a model for realizing her dream of
founding an enclosed monastery where the primitive Carmelite rule of
poverty, prayer, and solitude would be observed and an apostolate of
prayer for the Church carried out. That model was the House of
Nazareth, where St. Joseph's silent, humble service of and contemplative intimacy with Jesus and Mary became the prototype of the
Teresian Carmel. St. Joseph fulfilled many roles in Teresa's life, and
she wanted her Carmelite daughters to benefit in the same way as she
did in all their needs, confidently appealing to St. Joseph for his help
with the spiritual and relational challenges they faced in cloistered
community life, in meeting the temporal needs of their monasteries,
and in traveling rough and often dangerous roads to make new foundations or conduct the order's business.

With her reform, Teresa's references to St. Joseph as her father
take on another level of meaning. It is customary for members of religious orders and congregations to refer to their founders as "our
Father" or "our Mother" because these individuals exercise a spiritual paternity or maternity by giving birth to the community's charism
that makes a unique contribution to the life of the Universal Church.
For their part, religious owe a debt of gratitude and affection to their
founder as a spiritual parent. The force of Teresa's application of the

appellation "father" to St. Joseph undoubtedly signified that he was not only her spiritual father, but also that of the reformed Carmel, which came to regard him as its founder.[32] Gracián declares: "This order recognizes as the founder of its reform the glorious St. Joseph because it was with his assistance that Mother Teresa carried out this reform. . . ."[33]

After Teresa's canonization (1622), some monasteries wanted to change their titular patron from St. Joseph to St. Teresa, but Teresa appeared to Venerable Isabel de Santo Domingo (1537-1623) and sternly admonished her: "Tell the provincial to remove my name from the monasteries and to restore the name of St. Joseph."[34] Traditionally the Carmelites were dedicated to the Virgin Mary under the title "Our Lady of Mt. Carmel." Now the order of the Virgin Mary also became the order of St. Joseph. Perhaps it might even be said that St. Joseph was the first saint of the Teresian Carmel. In any event, the primacy given St. Joseph by Teresa and her daughters and sons would reverberate far beyond Carmel, influencing not only other religious orders, such as the Visitation[35] and the church in Spain and in France, but also the Universal Church.

Francis founded the Visitation Order for women who wanted to live a hidden life of great devotion, but lacked the hardy constitution required to sustain the rigorous lifestyle of established monastic orders, such as Carmel. To underscore that hiddenness was the hallmark of the Visitation, Francis incorporated Colossians 3:3 into the profession ceremony: "You have died, and your life is hidden with Christ in God." Jane de Chantal attests that she meditated on this verse day and night, praying for the grace of a hidden life for her and the order.[36] Thus, the Visitation sought, above all, to imitate Jesus' hidden life, and St. Joseph, to whom this phase of the Savior's life was entrusted, perfectly modeled for these women this essential quality of their vowed life and vocation, just as he exemplified for Teresa and her nuns the contemplative spirit.

It is not a coincidence that Francis appeals to Colossians 3:3 as the lens through which he views the mystery of the essential hiddenness of St. Joseph's life and virtues.[37] For Francis, St. Joseph modeled the hidden ordinary, everyday virtues, what the bishop called the "little virtues," which are the very heart and essence of true devotion: purity of mind and body, poverty, humility before God, gentleness toward neighbor, constancy, courage, perseverance, obedience to the Word of God, charity of judgment (cf. *Introduction to the Devout Life*, Part 3, chs. 1-2).

As is well known, Francis insisted on the universal call to holiness four centuries before the Second Vatican Council (1962-65). He envisioned that the Church would be renewed by the cumulative effect of each person responding to this call by the faithful and loving fulfillment of the ordinary, day-to-day duties and responsibilities of his/her state of life, whether as married or single person, cleric, or vowed religious. The Salesian spiritual vision, therefore, was larger than the Visitation Order. For Francis, St. Joseph, specifically in his virtues, perfectly models the Salesian spiritual vision, making him the first "Salesian saint," while he was also the father, founder, and first saint of the Teresian Carmel.

---

[1]   Quoted in Alphonse Vermeylen, *Sainte Thérèse en France au XVIIe siècle, 1600-1660* (Louvain: Publications Universitaires, 1958), 24.

[2]   All references to Teresa's works are to *The Collected Works of St. Teresa of Ávila,* trans. Kieran Kavanaugh, O.C.D., and Otilio Rodríguez, O.C.D., 3 vols. (Washington, D.C.: Institute of Carmelite Studies Publications, 1976-85): vol. 1, *The Book of Her Life, Spiritual Testimonies, Soliloquies;* vol. 2, *The Way of Perfection, Meditations on the Song of Songs, The Interior Castle;* vol. 3, *The Book of Her Foundations, Minor Works.* Teresa would subsequently expand this mission to include the rescue of souls being lost in

the New World through ignorance of the Gospel: see *Foundations*, 1.7-8.

3   See, e.g., Vermeylen, 25-27, and Barbara B. Diefendorf, *From Penitence to Charity: Pious Women and the Catholic Reformation in Paris* (New York: Oxford University Press, 2004), 95-96.

4   John Bossy, *Peace in the Post-Reformation*, The Birkbeck Lectures 1995 (New York: Cambridge University Press, 1998), 37.

5   Fourteen saints were canonized in the seventeenth century. Most can be gathered into one of two clusters. Six saints were canonized during Francis's lifetime: Charles Borromeo in 1610, Ignatius Loyola, Francis Xavier, Philip Neri, Isidore of Madrid, and Teresa of Ávila in 1622. After a lengthy hiatus, a second cluster was canonized between 1664 and 1671, with Francis being canonized in 1665. See R. Po-Chia Hsia, *The World of Catholic Renewal 1540-1770* (New York: Cambridge University Press, 1998), 122-37.

6   See Elisabeth Stopp's masterful essay "Spanish Links: St. Francis de Sales and St. Teresa of Ávila," in her *A Man to Heal Differences: Essays and Talks on St. Francis de Sales* (Philadelphia: Saint Joseph's University Press, 1997), 171-82. There have been a number of comparative studies of Teresa and Francis; for our purposes the most important are Vermeylen, and Pierre Sérouet, O.C.D., *De la vie dévote à la vie mystique: Sainte Thérèse d'Ávila, Saint François de Sales,* Études Carmélitaines (Paris: Desclée de Brouwer, 1958).

7   Diefendorf, 103.

8   Stopp, 176.

9   Stopp, 176-77.

10   On the French translations of Teresa's writings and works about her, see Vermeylen, 41-65, and Sérouet, 99-109. On the matter of Francis's reading of these sources in Spanish, Stopp sums up the state of the question: "[Francis] did not, at that point [1601-1602], as yet read Spanish fluently, though later on, when Spanish soldiers were for years stationed at Annecy and also in Turin, Francis de Sales's court of the Duke of Savoy, he made friends and disciples among the Spaniards and acquired a good speaking knowledge of the language" (176).

11   Stopp, 173.

12   See Joseph F. Chorpenning, O.S.F.S., introduction to his trans. and ed. of Francis de Sales, *Sermon Texts on Saint Joseph* (Toronto: Peregrina Publishing Co., 2000), 11-62, esp. 31, and 56-57, note 41.

13   Sérouet, 353, citing the testimony given by Jean-Baptiste Gard, a canon of

the Annecy cathedral chapter, in July 1656 for the second process of inquiry for Francis's canonization. In this connection, a recent study has demonstrated that Teresa came to be regarded in seventeenth-century France as the founder of devotion to St. Joseph: see Bernard Dompnier, "Thérèse d'Ávila et la dévotion française à saint Joseph au XVII⁰ siècle," *Revue d'Histoire de l'Église de France* 90, no. 224 (janvier-juin 2004): 175-90.

¹⁴   Sérouet, 353.

¹⁵   Efrén de la Madre de Dios, O.C.D., "Posibles influencias josefinas ambientales en Santa Teresa," *Estudios Josefinos* 18, nos. 34-35 (1964): 243-50, and Simeón de la Sagrada Familia, O.C.D., "Una nueva fuente del josefinismo de Santa Teresa," *Estudios Josefinos* 57, no. 114 (2003): 179-215.

¹⁶   See Simeón Tomás Fernández, O.C.D., "Las *Josefinas* de Bernardino de Laredo (1535) y de Andrés de Soto (1593), franciscanos," *Cahiers de Joséphologie* 25 (1977): 223-54, esp. 242-48.

¹⁷   Efrén de la Madre de Dios, 248-49. The way was paved for this effort more than a half century earlier when the polymath and scholar Alonso de Madrigal, "el Tostado" (c. 1400-55), a native of Ávila, set forth the basis of devotion to St. Joseph, treating extensively and profoundly the question of his marriage to Mary and his ministry as earthly father of Jesus, the foundation of all his prerogatives. See Ángel Luis, C.Ss.R., "Matrimonio y paternidad de San José según El Tostado," *Estudios Josefinos* 12, no. 24 (1958): 231-55.

¹⁸   Bartolomé M.ᵃ Xiberta, O. Carm., "Flores josefinas en la liturgia carmelitana antigua," *Estudios Josefinos* 18, nos. 34-35 (1964): 301-19.

¹⁹   See Francis de Sales, *Sermon Texts on St. Joseph.*

²⁰   Sérouet, 353, note 3.

²¹   I am grateful to my confrère Fr. Jean Gayet, O.S.F.S., for sharing with me his unpublished paper on the church of St. Joseph, which the bishop of Annecy renamed for St. Francis de Sales in 1923 to mark the third centenary of his death.

²²   On Francis and the *Spiritual Exercises*, see, e.g., Stopp, 171; F. Charmot, S.J., *Ignatius Loyola and Francis de Sales: Two Masters, One Spirituality,* trans. Sr. M. Renelle, S.S.N.D. (St. Louis: Herder, 1966); and Wendy M. Wright, "The Ignatian -Salesian Imagination and Familied Life," in *The Holy Family in Art and Devotion,* ed. Joseph F. Chorpenning, O.S.F.S. (Philadelphia: Saint Joseph's University Press, 1998), 104-109.

²³   On the second week of the *Exercises,* see Peter-Hans Kolvenbach, S.J., "Do

Not Hide the Hidden Life of Christ," *Secretariatus Spiritualitatis Ignatianae: Triannual Review of Ignatian Spirituality* 24, no. 3 (1993): 11-25.

24 Sérouet, 353, note 3.

25 St. Francis de Sales, *Selected Letters,* trans. with an introduction by Elisabeth Stopp (New York: Harper & Brothers, 1960), 138 (letter to Baronne de Chantal of 24 July 1607).

26 Sérouet, 353, note 3.

27 See William V. Hudon, introduction to his trans. and ed. of Lorenzo Scupoli, *Spiritual Combat,* in *Theatine Spirituality: Selected Writings,* Classics of Western Spirituality (New York: Paulist Press, 1996), 1-65, esp. 45-46.

28 Andrew Doze, *Saint Joseph: Shadow of the Father,* trans. Florestine Audett, R.J.M. (New York: Alba House, 1992), 16.

29 See, e.g., Francis L. Filas, S.J., *Joseph: The Man Closest to Jesus. The Complete Life, Theology and Devotional History of St. Joseph* (Boston: St. Paul Editions, 1962), 502-503, and *St. Bernardine's Sermon on St. Joseph,* trans. Eric May, O.F.M.Cap. (Paterson, N.J.: St. Anthony's Guild, 1947), 39.

30 Bernard Dompnier, "Les religieux et saint Joseph dans la France de la première moitié du XVIIᵉᵐᵉ siècle," *Siècles: Cahiers du Centre d'Histoire "Espaces et Cultures," Religieux, saints et dévotions: France et Pologne, XIIIᵉᵐᵉ-XVIIᵉᵐᵉ siècles,* no. 16 (2003): 57-75, esp 63-65, and "Thérèse d'Ávila et la dévotion française à saint Joseph," 181.

31 *Sermon Texts on St. Joseph,* 125-26.

32 Lucinio del Santísimo Sacramento, O.C.D., "La paternidad espiritual de S. José en la Orden del Carmen," *Estudios Josefinos* 6 (1952): 80-108, esp. 89, and José Antonio del Niño Jesús, O.C.D., "San José, fundador de la reforma teresiana," *Estudios Josefinos* 18, nos. 34-35 (1964): 339-53.

33 *Just Man, Husband of Mary, Guardian of Christ: An Anthology of Readings from Jerónimo Gracián's "Summary of the Excellencies of St. Joseph" (1597),* trans. and ed., with an introductory essay and commentary by Joseph F. Chorpenning, O.S.F.S. (Philadelphia: Saint Joseph's University Press, 1993), 242.

34 Quoted in Lucinio del Santísimo Sacramento, 102-103, and José Antonio del Niño Jesús, 352.

35 See, e.g., Bernard Dompnier, "La Visitation, saint François de Sales et la dévotion à saint Joseph," a paper given in 2002 as part of the celebration by the Académie salésienne in Annecy of the 400th anniversary of the episco-

pal ordination of St. Francis de Sales, and to be published in 2006.

[36] Elisabeth Stopp, *Madame de Chantal: Portrait of a Saint* (Westminster, Md.: Newman Press, 1963), 141. Also see Stopp's essay "Hiddenness: A Key Factor," in her *Hidden in God: Essays and Talks on St. Jane Frances de Chantal,* ed. Terence O'Reilly (Philadelphia: Saint Joseph's University Press, 1999), 109-15.

[37] *Sermon Texts on St. Joseph,* 91, 114-20.